JBoss™

A Developer's Notebook™

Other Java™ resources from O'Reilly

Related titles
Eclipse
Eclipse Cookbook™
Head First EJB™
Head First Design Patterns
Hibernate: A Developer's Notebook™
Java™ Enterprise in a Nutshell

Java™ in a Nutshell
Real World Web Services
Spring: A Developer's Notebook™
Tomcat: The Definitive Guide
Web Logic: The Definitive Guide

Java Books Resource Center
java.oreilly.com is a complete catalog of O'Reilly's books on Java and related technologies, including sample chapters and code examples.

OnJava.com is a one-stop resource for enterprise Java developers, featuring news, code recipes, interviews, weblogs, and more.

Conferences
O'Reilly brings diverse innovators together to nurture the ideas that spark revolutionary industries. We specialize in documenting the latest tools and systems, translating the innovator's knowledge into useful skills for those in the trenches. Visit *conferences.oreilly.com* for our upcoming events.

Safari Bookshelf (*safari.oreilly.com*) is the premier online reference library for programmers and IT professionals. Conduct searches across more than 1,000 books. Subscribers can zero in on answers to time-critical questions in a matter of seconds. Read the books on your Bookshelf from cover to cover or simply flip to the page you need. Try it today with a free trial.

JBoss™

A Developer's Notebook™

Norman Richards and Sam Griffith, Jr.

O'REILLY®

Beijing · Cambridge · Farnham · Köln · Sebastopol · Tokyo

JBoss™: A Developer's Notebook™
by Norman Richards and Sam Griffith, Jr.

Copyright © 2005 O'Reilly Media, Inc. All rights reserved.
Printed in the United States of America.

Published by O'Reilly Media, Inc., 1005 Gravenstein Highway North, Sebastopol, CA 95472.

Editor:	Mike Loukides
Production Editor:	Colleen Gorman
Cover Designer:	Edie Freedman
Interior Designer:	David Futato

Printing History:

June 2005:	First Edition.

ISBN: 978-0-596-10007-0
[LSI]   [2011-08-12]

Contents

The Developer's Notebook Series

So, you've managed to pick this book up. Cool. Really, I'm excited about that! Of course, you may be wondering why these books have the odd-looking, college notebook sort of cover. I mean, this is O'Reilly, right? Where are the animals? And, really, do you *need* another series? Couldn't this just be a cookbook? How about a nutshell, or one of those cool hacks books that seems to be everywhere? The short answer is that a developer's notebook is none of those things—in fact, it's such an important idea that we came up with an entirely new look and feel, complete with cover, fonts, and even some notes in the margin. This is all a result of trying to get something into your hands you can actually use.

It's my strong belief that while the nineties were characterized by everyone wanting to learn everything (Why not? We all had six-figure incomes from dot-com companies), the new millennium is about information pain. People don't have time (or the income) to read through 600 page books, often learning 200 things, of which only about 4 apply to their current job. It would be much nicer to just sit near one of the uber-coders and look over his shoulder, wouldn't it? To ask the guys that are neck-deep in this stuff why they chose a particular method, how they performed this one tricky task, or how they avoided that threading issue when working with piped streams. The thinking has always been that books can't serve that particular need—they can inform, and let you decide, but ultimately a coder's mind was something that couldn't really be captured on a piece of paper.

This series says that assumption is patently wrong—and we aim to prove it.

A Developer's Notebook is just what it claims to be: the often-frantic scribbling and notes that a true-blue alpha geek mentally makes when working with a new language, API, or project. It's the no-nonsense code that solves problems, stripped of page-filling commentary that often serves more as a paperweight than an epiphany. It's hackery, focused not on what is nifty or might be fun to do when you've got some free time (when's the last time that happened?), but on what you need to simply "make it work." This isn't a lecture, folks—it's a lab. If you want a lot of concept, architecture, and UML diagrams, I'll happily and proudly point you to our animal and nutshell books. If you want every answer to every problem under the sun, our omnibus cookbooks are killer. And if you are into arcane and often quirky uses of technology, hacks books simply rock. But if you're a coder, down to your core, and you just want to get on with it, then you want a Developer's Notebook. Coffee stains and all, this is from the mind of a developer to yours, barely even cleaned up enough for print. I hope you enjoy it...we sure had a good time writing them.

Notebooks Are...

Example-driven guides

As you'll see in the "Organization" section, developer's notebooks are built entirely around example code. You'll see code on nearly every page, and it's code that *does something*—not trivial "Hello World!" programs that aren't worth more than the paper they're printed on.

Aimed at developers

Ever read a book that seems to be aimed at pointy-haired bosses, filled with buzzwords, and feels more like a marketing manifesto than a programming text? We have too—and these books are the antithesis of that. In fact, a good notebook is incomprehensible to someone who can't program (don't say we didn't warn you!), and that's just the way it's supposed to be. But for developers...it's as good as it gets.

Actually enjoyable to work through

Do you really have time to sit around reading something that isn't any fun? If you do, then maybe you're into thousand-page language references—but if you're like the rest of us, notebooks are a much better fit. Practical code samples, terse dialogue centered around practical examples, and even some humor here and there—these are the ingredients of a good developer's notebook.

About doing, not talking about doing

If you want to read a book late at night without a computer nearby, these books might not be that useful. The intent is that you're coding as you go along, knee deep in bytecode. For that reason, notebooks talk code, code, code. Fire up your editor before digging in.

Notebooks Aren't...

Lectures

We don't let just anyone write a developer's notebook—you've got to be a bona fide programmer, and preferably one who stays up a little too late coding. While full-time writers, academics, and theorists are great in some areas, these books are about programming in the trenches, and are filled with instruction, not lecture.

Filled with conceptual drawings and class hierarchies

This isn't a nutshell (there, we said it). You won't find 100-page indices with every method listed, and you won't see full-page UML diagrams with methods, inheritance trees, and flow charts. What you will find is page after page of source code. Are you starting to sense a recurring theme?

Long on explanation, light on application

It seems that many programming books these days have three, four, or more chapters before you even see any working code. I'm not sure who has authors convinced that it's good to keep a reader waiting this long, but it's not anybody working on *this* series. We believe that if you're not coding within ten pages, something's wrong. These books are also chock-full of practical application, taking you from an example in a book to putting things to work on your job, as quickly as possible.

Organization

Developer's Notebooks try to communicate different information than most books, and as a result, are organized differently. They do indeed have chapters, but that's about as far as the similarity between a notebook and a traditional programming book goes. First, you'll find that all the headings in each chapter are organized around a specific task. You'll note that we said *task*, not *concept*. That's one of the important things to get about these books—they are first and foremost about doing something. Each of these headings represents a single *lab*. A lab is just what it sounds like—steps to accomplish a specific goal. In fact, that's the first heading you'll see under each lab: "How do I do that?" This is the central question of each lab, and you'll find lots of down-and-dirty code and detail in these sections. Many labs offer alternatives and address common questions about different approaches to similar problems. These are the "What about..." sections, which will help give each task some context within the programming big picture.

And one last thing—on many pages, you'll find notes scrawled in the margins of the page. These aren't for decoration; they contain tips, tricks, insights from the developers of a product, and sometimes even a little humor, just to keep you going. These notes represent part of the overall communication flow—getting you as close to reading the mind of the developer-author as we can. Hopefully they'll get you that much closer to feeling like you are indeed learning from a master.

And most of all, remember—these books are...

All Lab, No Lecture

—Brett McLaughlin, Series Creator

Preface

In 1999, a couple of guys got together and decided to start an open source EJB container project. Six years later, we have JBoss 4.0, and the difference between that early version and this one is a lot greater than a few version numbers might suggest. While JBoss is still an open source community-driven project, it is much more than just an EJB container. JBoss 4.0 is a full J2EE 1.4-certified application server. It is competitive with proprietary application servers in terms of features and quality, and has risen to be the number one application server in terms of overall market share. There's definitely something special about it.

JBoss isn't any ordinary open source project. It's one of the few open source projects that have found commercial success without betraying their open source roots. JBoss is backed by JBoss, Inc., a successful and rapidly growing company with more than 100 full-time employees fueling the continued development of the project. Although JBoss is freely available for any purpose, it is backed by a real company that provides support and training for those who need the reassurance of having strong vendor backing.

JBoss isn't any ordinary J2EE application server either. JBoss has been at the forefront of innovation, pioneering the lightweight microkernel and pluggable services style of development that is popular today. While JBoss can't take sole credit for smart proxies, interceptor stacks, or any of the other technology tracks it is famous for, there's little doubt that JBoss significantly advanced the state of the art and continues to be on the forefront of J2EE.

JBoss isn't just a J2EE server. Most people come to JBoss because they want a J2EE application server, but JBoss's dynamic architecture allows it to go well beyond J2EE. Although JBoss provides a fully certified J2EE container, you are free to alter the services provided to make J2EE work the way you want. You can even throw J2EE away completely, working at a lower services level or at a higher level using technologies such as AOP and Hibernate. You can make JBoss as heavy or as light as you need it to be. You can stick to the J2EE specification for maximum portability, or you can rewrite the rules to obtain maximum agility and performance. With JBoss, the choice is yours!

If you think of JBoss as just an ordinary application server, we hope that in reading this book, you'll begin to feel the same sense of excitement we feel about it. We hope you'll see that JBoss isn't a complex product that you curse at under your breath while wishing for a simpler way to get your work done. It is a flexible platform that you can use to simplify your life, leaving you more time to focus on what is really important: your applications.

Conventions Used in This Book

The following typographical conventions are used in this book:

Plain text

> Indicates menu titles, menu options, menu buttons, and keyboard accelerators (such as Alt and Ctrl).

Italic

> Indicates new terms, URLs, email addresses, filenames, file extensions, pathnames, directories, and Unix utilities.

`Constant width`

> Indicates commands, options, switches, variables, attributes, keys, functions, types, classes, namespaces, methods, modules, properties, parameters, values, objects, events, event handlers, XML tags, HTML tags, macros, the contents of files, or the output from commands.

`Constant width bold`

> Shows commands or other text that should be typed literally by the user.

`Constant width italic`

> Shows text that should be replaced with user-supplied values.

TIP

Indicates a tip, suggestion, or general note.

Using Code Examples

This book is here to help you get your job done. In general, you may use the code in this book in your programs and documentation. You do not need to contact us for permission unless you're reproducing a significant portion of the code. For example, writing a program that uses several chunks of code from this book does not require permission. Selling or distributing a CD-ROM of examples from O'Reilly books *does* require permission. Answering a question by citing this book and quoting example code does not require permission. Incorporating a significant amount of example code from this book into your product's documentation *does* require permission.

We appreciate, but do not require, attribution. An attribution usually includes the title, author, publisher, and ISBN. For example: "*JBoss: A Developer's Notebook*, by Norman Richards and Sam Griffith, Jr. Copyright 2005 O'Reilly Media, Inc., 0-596-10007-8."

If you feel your use of code examples falls outside fair use or the permission given above, feel free to contact us at *permissions@oreilly.com*.

Comments and Questions

Please address comments and questions concerning this book to the publisher:

> O'Reilly Media, Inc.
> 1005 Gravenstein Highway North
> Sebastopol, CA 95472
> (800) 998-9938 (in the United States or Canada)
> (707) 829-0515 (international or local)
> (707) 829-0104 (fax)

We have a web page for this book, where we list errata, examples, and any additional information. You can access this page at:

> *http://www.oreilly.com/catalog/jbossadn*

To comment or ask technical questions about this book, send email to:

> *bookquestions@oreilly.com*

For more information about our books, conferences, Resource Centers, and the O'Reilly Network, see our web site at:

http://www.oreilly.com

Safari® Enabled

 When you see a Safari® enabled icon on the cover of your favorite technology book, that means the book is available online through the O'Reilly Network Safari Bookshelf.

Safari offers a solution that's better than e-Books. It's a virtual library that lets you easily search thousands of top tech books, cut and paste code samples, download chapters, and find quick answers when you need the most accurate, current information. Try it free at *http://safari.oreilly.com*.

Acknowledgments

Writing a book such as this is never an easy task, and we couldn't have done it without help from many, many people. We'd like to thank everyone at O'Reilly who helped get this book out. We'd like to thank Colleen Gorman and Audrey Doyle, for turning edits around so quickly. We'd especially like to thank our editor, Mike Loukides, for believing in the book and giving us the opportunity to write it.

We are particularly grateful to everyone who read early drafts of the book and gave us feedback: Chris Bono, Rhys Ulerich, Alex McCarrier, and Ivelin Ivanov. While we strove to make the book as good as we could from the start, you guys helped us smooth out the rough edges for everyone else. Thanks!

Finally, we'd like to thank the entire JBoss community for producing the finest Java application server on the market. Thank you for making the best application server out there, and for giving us something to write about.

Norman's Acknowledgments

Vincent... Thank you for not complaining when I needed to spend a little more time working on the book. I know I don't always do a good job balancing work and free time, but I do try.

Sarah... You've been an inspiration to me these last few months, and you have given me the energy I needed to keep at it. Good luck with your own book. I really hope to see it in print someday soon. I know you will be a big success!

Chris... Thanks for the help with the review. You done a great jorb!

Pyoung-Gyu... Thanks, because if I didn't acknowledge you here, I know you'd get mad at me.

Julie... Thanks for still being a friend. Sorry the lottery number didn't work out last time. I guess I'm not psychic after all.

Sunny... It's good to have you back in Texas.

Margot... Thanks for finally giving me closure.

JBoss... Working for JBoss has been a dream come true. Some days I can barely believe I'm getting paid to work on open source software, especially something as big as JBoss. I'd like to thank Marc and Andy for giving me my break here. And, I'd like to thank all the guys in the Austin office (Ivelin, Ryan, Steve, Michael, Clebert, and Charles) for making it an office I don't dread going to.

I'd like to thank O'Reilly for coming up with a great book format that lets me scribble in the margins like this.

Austin... Thanks for being the greatest city in the world to live in. It is truly the Promised Land, a land flowing with burritos and free WiFi. Thanks for being a place that fosters such a vibrant technical community. It has made all the difference.

Sam's Acknowledgments

This is so much like the Academy Awards. Do I only have only one minute? I've written this at least three times and, well, it's always long, so I'm just leaving it this time. Thanks go to...

Norman... I wouldn't have had the chance to work on this if you hadn't asked me to participate and given me a chance to try writing. Now I know that for me, public speaking is much easier! I also appreciate you mentoring me in the writing of this book, and the fact that you cleaned up my work to make it flow. Thanks a lot.

Morgan... You've been an inspiration since before you were born. Since last fall when Norman and I started this you've been patient while I had to write and you played. From time to time, you would ask me what I was doing, and why. The "what" you will be able to see in the physical book itself. The "why" is a bit harder to explain, but it's all of these reasons, and more: because Norman asked me to, because I wanted to see my name in the Library of Congress, because I wanted to go to the bookstore and see my name on a book instead of in one, but mostly because I wanted you to be able to say one day that your dad wrote a book and for you to be proud of me! I love you, Morgan, and I hope when you're old enough to read this you understand what a motivator you are to me in my life. I hope you grow up strong and healthy and that I can be as good a father as you are a son. I love you heaps and heaps!

Mom and Dad... For always believing in me, even when you didn't understand what I was doing or where I was going. I'm glad you invested in my future so long ago with the TI-994A, and then with an original Macintosh. Those investments paid off pretty well! I love you both!

Susan... You have provided and continue to provide inspiration as a friend. Things you've said and done were bigger than the moment or the time. Thank you for those times and moments. Thank you for being a friend. You'll always be with me.

Seeing as this may be the only time I ever get to do this, there are lots of other people that I need to thank as well. These people have contributed to my growth as a mentor, trainer, programmer, friend, and person. I don't have space to say why, but I want to thank them. So, here they are, in no particular order: Grady Clendenning, Joyce Crocker, Tony Gibson, Christine Kungel, Melba Sanchez, Alex Nghiem, Kevin Wittkopf, Perry Anderson, Laura Whitehead, Blaine Buxton, Rose Wang, Leroy Mattingly, Deb Ayers, David Shelor, Ron Smith, Scott Shattuck, Lance Bledsoe, Ray Garton, William Edney, Wayne Hearn, John Head, Tina Gilbert, Ross Gorde, Dick Norton, Geoff Kaiser, Sunny Adams, Allen Keirn, Andy Littman, Mark Morrison, Kelly Edwards, Tee McNamara, Ron Smith, Scott Boyd, Greg Marriot, Jay Zaback, Andrew Donahoe, Larry Turcotte, Bill Dudney, Mr. and Mrs. Jackson, the Mauck family, Rebecca Redwood, and finally, the big guy upstairs. Thanks to all of you. I'm sure I've left off someone, and to you I send my thanks as well. I lost my address book a few years ago, so I'm going from memory. Also, if I misspelled your name, I'm sorry 'bout that, my memory is not what it used to be.

My friends will tell you I'm a very adept talker!

Finally, work on this book was fun, but at the same time it was a hard task for me. I tend to want to write like I talk.

That style of writing leads to run-on sentences. Mike, our editor, would remind me from time to time in his feedback about run-ons, and I've slowly gotten better at avoiding them. Although writing is not easy or natural to me yet, working on this book has served as a real motivator for me to try and write more. Some quotes that sum up my feelings about working on this book:

> If a man is called to be a street sweeper, he should sweep streets even as Michelangelo painted, or Beethoven composed music, or Shakespeare wrote poetry. He should sweep streets so well that all the hosts of Heaven and Earth will pause to say, here lived a great street sweeper who did his job well.
>
> —Martin Luther King

All labor that uplifts humanity has dignity and importance and should be undertaken with painstaking excellence.

—Martin Luther King

I hope you, the reader, find this book to be an excellent piece of work, as Norman and I have tried to do our work well. We both found ourselves slammed at work, busy during holiday season and seemingly always short on time. But with all that and a lot of motivation from our editor, I think we've created something we can be very proud of.

Last, but not least, remember that the answer is 42!

CHAPTER 1

Installing and Running JBoss

We will start by installing JBoss and getting the server up and running. You'll be surprised by how easy it is to work with JBoss. It doesn't matter whether you're on Linux, Mac, or Windows; you can get the full JBoss application server running in just a few minutes. So, let's get going.

In this chapter:
- *Installing the Server*
- *Starting Up JBoss*
- *Examining the Server (JMX Console)*
- *Shutting Down the Server*
- *Specifying a Server Configuration*
- *Creating a New Configuration*

Installing the Server

Installing JBoss is so easy that new users often think they are missing something. But don't mistake this simplicity for lack of power or configurability. Before we get started, you'll need to make sure you have either Java 1.4 or Java 1.5 installed on your machine. That's the only prerequisite for JBoss 4, so if you are all set we'll get started.

How do I do that?

You can download the latest JBoss version, currently 4.0.2, from the JBoss download page at *http://www.jboss.org/downloads/index*. Once you choose the version of the JBoss application server you want, you'll be taken to the SourceForge.net page to do the actual download. When you get there select one of the prebuilt binary distributions. For JBoss 4. 0.2 look for a file named *jboss-4.0.2.zip*. You'll also see *jboss-.4.0.2.tar.gz* and *jboss-4.0.2.tar.bz2* archives. If either of those formats works better for your platform, feel free to use it instead.

We use Java 1.4 in most examples, but there should be no differences if you use Java 1.5. JRE install.

Before JBoss 4.0.2, JBoss required a full JDK installation to compile JSP files. As of Version 4.0.2, Tomcat ships with its own Java compiler, so JBoss only requires a JRE install.

Many of the releases have service packs, which are marked with the *sp* designation. Always choose the latest service pack release for the version

If you are on a
Unix machine, we
suggest sticking
with the .tar.gz
release to make
sure file permis-
sions are
preserved
accurately.

you are downloading. You might also see source code releases marked with the -src suffix, as well as *RC* (release candidate) and *DR* (developer release) versions of the server. Ignore those for now and stick to the production binaries. In this book we will work from the *jboss-4.0.2.tar.gz* release.

Uncompress the download into the directory where you want JBoss installed, using the appropriate tool for your platform. We put the server into */Users/samjr/jboss-4.0.2*; here's the *bin* directory of the installed server:

```
[bin]$ pwd
/Users/samjr/jboss-4.0.2/bin
[bin]$ ls
classpath.sh          jboss_init_suse.sh    run.sh          twiddle.bat
deployer.bat          run.bat               shutdown.bat    twiddle.jar
deployer.sh           run.conf              shutdown.jar    twiddle.sh
jboss_init_redhat.sh  run.jar               shutdown.sh
```

If you don't have
a good zip tool,
you can always use
the Java jar
program to
expand the zip
archive.

What just happened?

You just installed one of the most powerful application servers available today. Really powerful tools usually need much more setup and configuration, but not JBoss. Now, you're ready to start it up.

What about...

...if I installed JBoss on another box on my network?

You will want to check the firewall settings on that machine. Specifically, you'll want to make sure that port 8080 is open so that you'll be able to access the JBoss web server to test it out. If you installed JBoss locally you shouldn't have to worry about this.

WARNING

Be careful about installing JBoss on a machine that might be visible from the Internet. JBoss ships in an insecure state that allows external access to server management features.

Starting Up JBoss

You might expect it to be complicated and time consuming to configure the server and get it running for the first time. JBoss is indeed a complex server, but it's simple to run, configure, and maintain. Later in the book we will see the different kinds of configuration and maintenance options, but for now let's just get JBoss up and running.

How do I do that?

To start JBoss, you'll need to use the run script in the *bin* directory of the server. There is a *run.sh* script for use on Unix machines and a *run.bat* file for Windows. When you run the script, you'll see something like the following output:

```
[bin]$ ./run.sh
===============================================================

  JBoss Bootstrap Environment

  JBOSS_HOME: /Users/samjr/jboss-4.0.2RC1

  JAVA: java

  JAVA_OPTS: -server -Xms128m -Xmx128m -Dprogram.name=run.sh

  CLASSPATH: /Users/samjr/jboss-4.0.2RC1/bin/run.jar:/lib/tools.jar

===============================================================

05:02:58,197 INFO  [Server] Starting JBoss (MX MicroKernel)...
05:02:58,230 INFO  [Server] Release ID: JBoss [Zion] 4.0.2RC1 (build:
CVSTag=JBoss_4_0_2_RC1 date=200503140913)
05:02:58,232 INFO  [Server] Home Dir: /Users/samjr/jboss-4.0.2RC1
05:02:58,233 INFO  [Server] Home URL: file:/Users/samjr/jboss-4.0.2RC1/
05:02:58,235 INFO  [Server] Library URL: file:/Users/samjr/jboss-4.0.2RC1/
lib/
05:02:58,238 INFO  [Server] Patch URL: null
05:02:58,256 INFO  [Server] Server Name: default
05:02:58,258 INFO  [Server] Server Home Dir: /Users/samjr/jboss-4.0.2RC1/
server/default
05:02:58,259 INFO  [Server] Server Home URL: file:/Users/samjr/jboss-4.0.
2RC1/server/default/
05:02:58,261 INFO  [Server] Server Data Dir: /Users/samjr/jboss-4.0.2RC1/
server/default/data
05:02:58,262 INFO  [Server] Server Temp Dir: /Users/samjr/jboss-4.0.2RC1/
server/default/tmp
05:02:58,264 INFO  [Server] Server Config URL: file:/Users/samjr/jboss-4.0.
2RC1/server/default/conf/
05:02:58,265 INFO  [Server] Server Library URL: file:/Users/samjr/jboss-4.0.
2RC1/server/default/lib/
05:02:58,267 INFO  [Server] Root Deployment Filename: jboss-service.xml
05:02:58,324 INFO  [Server] Starting General Purpose Architecture (GPA)...

   [Lots of startup output removed for brevity]

05:04:05,834 INFO  [TomcatDeployer] deploy, ctxPath=/quote, warUrl=file:/
Users/samjr/jboss-4.0.2RC1/server/default/tmp/deploy/tmp14739quote.war/
05:04:06,348 INFO  [Http11Protocol] Starting Coyote HTTP/1.1 on http-0.0.0.
0-8080
05:04:06,868 INFO  [ChannelSocket] JK2: ajp13 listening on /0.0.0.0:8009
```

Most of the services in JBoss log output as they start up. Additional log output is available in the server.log file.

```
05:04:06,956 INFO  [JkMain] Jk running ID=0 time=0/199  config=null
05:04:07,092 INFO  [Server] JBoss (MX MicroKernel) [4.0.2RC1 (build:
CVSTag=JBoss_4_0_2_RC1 date=200503140913)] Started in 1m:7s:977ms
```

That's it! JBoss is up and running. Right there on that last line we have full confirmation that it's up. But just to make sure, go to *http://localhost: 8080/* in your browser. You should see the JBoss welcome page that looks similar to Figure 1-1.

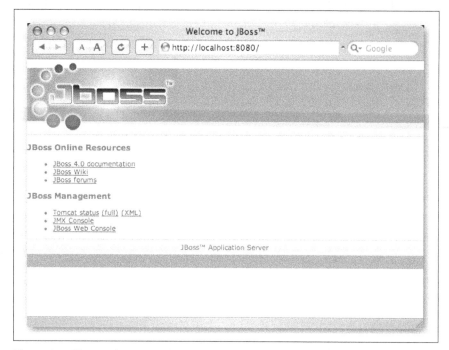

Figure 1-1. JBoss welcome page

Congratulations! Your JBoss server is now running.

Examining the Server (JMX Console)

The JBoss application server provides a management application that lets you see and manage the services that are deployed and running inside the server. JBoss itself is implemented as a microkernel composed of managed beans (MBeans). The MBeans that are visible provide you a way to manage the resources and applications that are deployed on your application server. This allows you to monitor and modify applications and their usage. You can see what MBeans you have through the JMX

Console. The JMX Console organizes the MBeans by the domain, as well by type (service, database, etc.). When you select an MBean you are taken to a page where you can view and edit attributes or invoke the operations of that MBean.

How do I do that?

You can get to the JBoss JMX Console by going to the main web page (*http://localhost:8080*) and choosing the JMX Console link. This will take you to the jmx-console web application at *http://localhost:8080/jmx-console*. When you're there, you'll see something like Figure 1-2.

You can manage all the JBoss services through the JMX Console. If you provide MBeans for your own services, you will see them here too.

Figure 1-2. JMX Console

JBoss provides an MBean that allows you to look at your server information. To do that now, scroll down in your browser until you get to the section for the *jboss.system* domain. You should see a link for this: *type=ServerInfo*. Choose that link and you'll see the ServerInfo MBean page. It will look something like Figure 1-3.

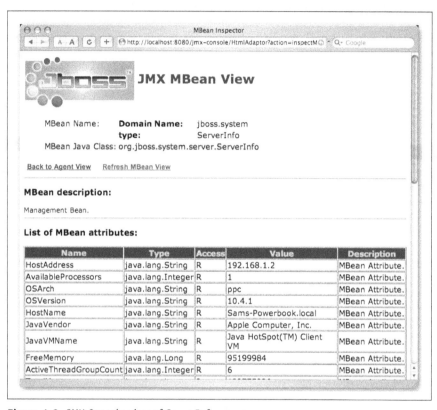

Figure 1-3. JMX Console view of ServerInfo

If you are feeling adventurous, look at some of the other MBeans and see what other types of information are exposed.

You can see what JVM JBoss is running on top of, what operating system it is running on, etc. That's useful information, especially if you are doing remote monitoring.

What just happened?

You opened the JMX Console on the JBoss server and viewed the ServerInfo MBean. You also saw that the MBeans are organized according to the domain they are in. While this might not seem like much now, it will come in handy as we work our way through the book.

Shutting Down the Server

Now that you know how to start the server and look at it using the JMX Console, you need to know how to shut it down properly. It's really pretty simple, so let's get to it.

How do I do that?

You can shut down the server in three ways:

- Use the JMX Console to go to the `jboss.system` domain and choose the `type=Server` MBean link. On the MBean page, scroll down to the operations section and click the "Invoke" button for the `shutdown( )` operation.
- Run the shutdown script for your platform in the same directory where you found the run script.
- Type **Ctrl-c** in the same console window where you started JBoss.

When JBoss is stopped, you'll see the following message:

```
03:50:02,412 INFO  [Server] Shutdown complete
```

You can verify that JBoss has stopped by trying to access the server in your web browser. You won't be able to connect because the server is not running anymore.

What just happened?

Just as you would expect, the application server shut down. You also learned three different ways to stop JBoss, and you got to see another useful MBean. Of those three ways, when should you use one or the other?

In development, the Ctrl-c option is the easiest because you will likely have an open terminal window running JBoss. However, if JBoss is running as a service, especially on a remote machine, you'll need to use one of the other options. If you have shell access to the machine, the shutdown script will work fine. You can also use the shutdown command to shut down a remote JBoss instance, but this requires a local JBoss installation and a few extra command-line arguments. For remote machines, it's often more convenient to just use the JMX Console. If you keep a bookmark set to the ServerInfo MBean, it can be a very quick process. In the end, each option serves the needs of different types of users, so just choose whatever is most convenient for you.

The shutdown script is in the bin directory with the startup script! The twiddle script is a program for "twiddling" with a remote JBoss server.

Specifying a Server Configuration

JBoss is not only powerful, it's also very configurable. At the center of JBoss is a JMX microkernel that manages the MBeans that control the various services in the server. The JBoss documentation describes the microkernel as a spine, and the analogy fits well. JBoss in its minimum configuration is like the brainstem sitting at the top of the spine. It provides all the core autonomic features (to steal some thunder from IBM's autonomic computing initiative). The spinal column is the attachment point for all the MBeans that want to talk to the brainstem and to each other over the spinal cord. This architecture provides a strong backbone to build on, but at the same time it can work at its most minimal state and still do amazing things. It makes JBoss useful for everything from very small, embedded applications all the way up to full-blown enterprise server applications, all on the same spinal column.

Having a flexible architecture is pointless unless you can make use of that flexibility. JBoss provides several different configurations that range from a barebones server with no J2EE capabilities to a superserver with more services than any single application could possibly use. Figure 1-4 shows the three standard server configurations.

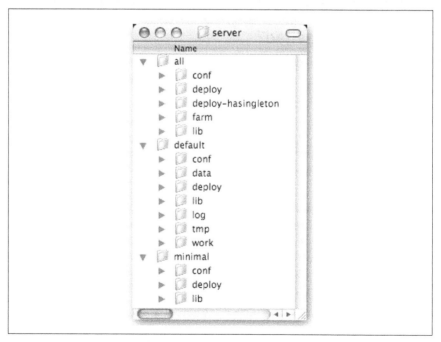

Figure 1-4. Server configurations

Here are descriptions of the server configurations:

minimal

> This configuration provides the bare services you might need in the simplest application: logging, JNDI naming services, and URL deployment scanning. You'd use this setup in tight memory situations, or when you want to use JMX to control exactly which MBeans are loaded, and when and how they are loaded. This configuration doesn't provide support for EJBs, web applications, JMS, or any other high-level services. It's just a raw microkernel waiting to be molded.

default

> This is a lightweight J2EE configuration; it's the one most people use. It provides most of the common J2EE services, but it doesn't include IIOP, JAXR, or clustering services, for example. These services can be added easily to this configuration.

all

> This configuration includes everything in JBoss. If you need any extra services not provided in the default configuration, this is the place to start. It's often easier to start from the all configuration and take out unwanted services than to start with the default configuration and add the desired services.

There is a huge difference in the size of these configurations. The minimal configuration can start up in just a few seconds, whereas it can take nearly a minute for the all configuration to completely start on a typical developer machine.

The all configuration includes everthing but the proverbial kitchen sink.

How do I do that?

You specify a particular configuration using the -c command to the run script. To run the minimal configuration, for example, use -c minimal.

Here is an example:

```
[bin]$ ./run.sh -c minimal
```

You can also use --configuration=minimal, if you prefer to use long configuration names.

Creating a New Configuration

You aren't limited to the three configurations JBoss provides. In fact, instead of having unneeded services loaded, wasting memory and CPU space, you can create your own JBoss configuration that has exactly what you need. It's actually quite easy to create a custom configuration.

How do I do that?

The easiest way to create your own configuration is to copy an existing one and then rename the folder to something that describes your configuration options. Once you've done that you can add any new JARs and resources to that new server configuration folder.

Let's say you want to create a new configuration based on minimal that you can add other services to later. You can copy the minimal server configuration folder to a new folder in the server folder and call it my_server_config. On Unix this would be cp -R minimal my_server_config.

You can run your new configuration like this:

```
[bin]$ ./run.sh -c my_server_config
```

The server will start up using your new configuration, and you'll see console output that looks like this:

```
==========================================================

JBoss Bootstrap Environment

JBOSS_HOME: /Users/samjr/jboss-4.0.2RC1

JAVA: java

JAVA_OPTS: -server -Xms128m -Xmx128m -Dprogram.name=run.sh

CLASSPATH: /Users/samjr/jboss-4.0.2RC1/bin/run.jar:/lib/tools.jar

==========================================================

05:49:22,213 INFO  [Server] Starting JBoss (MX MicroKernel)...
05:49:22,217 INFO  [Server] Release ID: JBoss [Zion] 4.0.2RC1 (build:
CVSTag=JBoss_4_0_2_RC1 date=200503140913)
05:49:22,220 INFO  [Server] Home Dir: /Users/samjr/jboss-4.0.2RC1
05:49:22,221 INFO  [Server] Home URL: file:/Users/samjr/jboss-4.0.2RC1/
05:49:22,223 INFO  [Server] Library URL: file:/Users/samjr/jboss-4.0.2RC1/lib/
05:49:22,226 INFO  [Server] Patch URL: null
05:49:22,244 INFO  [Server] **Server Name: my_server_config**
05:49:22,246 INFO  [Server] Server Home Dir: /Users/samjr/jboss-4.0.2RC1/
server/my_server_config
05:49:22,247 INFO  [Server] Server Home URL: file:/Users/samjr/jboss-4.0.
2RC1/server/my_server_config/
05:49:22,249 INFO  [Server] Server Data Dir: /Users/samjr/jboss-4.0.2RC1/
server/my_server_config/data
05:49:22,250 INFO  [Server] Server Temp Dir: /Users/samjr/jboss-4.0.2RC1/
server/my_server_config/tmp
05:49:22,251 INFO  [Server] Server Config URL: file:/Users/samjr/jboss-4.0.
2RC1/server/my_server_config/conf/
05:49:22,285 INFO  [Server] Server Library URL: file:/Users/samjr/jboss-4.0.
2RC1/server/my_server_config/lib/
05:49:22,287 INFO  [Server] Root Deployment Filename: jboss-service.xml
05:49:22,294 INFO  [Server] Starting General Purpose Architecture (GPA)...

    [More startup information]

05:50:44,641 INFO  [Server] JBoss (MX MicroKernel) [4.0.2RC1 (build:
CVSTag=JBoss_4_0_2_RC1 date=200503140913)] Started in 1m:21s:849ms
```

And with that, the new configuration is started.

What about...

...adding or removing services from the configuration?

While new configurations are nice simply as a way to work in an isolated sandbox, the original premise for creating a new configuration was to customize the set of services available. We'll need a bit more background to do that type of serious customization. But as we learn how to customize the services throughout this book, you'll be able to come back and apply those changes to your own configuration.

We hope you've seen how easy it is to get up and running and how easy it is to create new configurations of the JBoss server. The power is provided in a simple and configurable way. Congratulations for getting this far. Now let's move on to the next chapter and see how to package and deploy a simple application.

CHAPTER 2

Deploying an Application on JBoss

WAR stands for Web Application Archive.

In the last chapter we focused on getting the application server up and running. Now we will see how to build a simple web application, get it running on the server, and then monitor it. The pattern of build–install–test–monitor is standard in engineering; in this chapter, we'll see how to do those things in JBoss. The application titled "The Great Albert Einstein Quote Machine" demonstrates the deployment of a web application on JBoss while dispensing interesting quotes.

Getting Ant

Ant is a build tool made with Java in mind, allowing Java developers to have a tool that fits with the Java environment and mentality. It is an expandable, open source tool that is constantly being upgraded and extended to support the latest Java standards. One specific standard that we use in this chapter is the WAR file, which will allow us to package up our application. We'll learn more about what a WAR file is, and why it's important, in a little bit.

Ant has an active community of supporters who have helped make Ant the preferred build tool in the Java community (pun intended). With that in mind, we've chosen to use Ant for the examples in this book. At the end of this book, you too might be one of those supporters or contributors. So...

How do I do that?

Ant is provided in both source and binary form. For the examples and work we are doing in this book you'll only need the binaries. To get the binaries, go to *http://ant.apache.org/bindownload.cgi* and download a binary distribution. Choose a binary format that is appropriate for your system.

For more about Ant, check out Ant: The Definitive Guide (O'Reilly).

Once you've unpacked the download, you'll need to set the ANT_HOME environment variable to point at the directory in which you unpacked Ant, which is */Users/samjr/apache-ant-1.6.2* in this example. You also need to add Ant's *bin* directory to your command path. In this example it is */Users/samjr/apache-ant-1.6.2/bin*. You can find more information about configuring and installing Ant in the Ant manual, available online at *http://ant.apache.org/manual/*.

You can do a quick check to see if Ant is working by typing `ant -version` on the command line. You should see something like this:

```
[samjr]$ ant -version
Apache Ant version 1.6.2 compiled on July 16 2004
```

Creating and Packaging the Application

The application is the soon-to-be-classic "The Great Albert Einstein Quote Machine." The application is simple; it consists of five files, including the build file.

In this section we look at the required files for a simple JBoss web application, and the build file to package them up so that JBoss can run them.

How do I do that?

Since our application is a web application, it is packaged as a WAR file for deployment on the server. The WAR file has places for JSPs, HTML, libraries, and metadata (see Figure 2-1).

Let's look at the files that go into a WAR file; as we talk about each file we'll identify where it goes in the WAR file.

Figure 2-1. Standard WAR file structure

The first file is the core of our application, *quote.jsp*:

```
<%@ taglib prefix="c" uri="http://java.sun.com/jsp/jstl/core" %>
<%@ page import="java.util.ArrayList" %>
<%@ page import="java.util.Random" %>

<%
  //List of sayings
  String[] quotes = {
    "Before God we are all equally wise - and equally foolish",
    "I never think of the future - it comes soon enough",
    "Imagination is more important than knowledge...",
    "Reality is merely an illusion, albeit a very persistent one",
    "The important thing is not to stop questioning",
    "The secret to creativity is knowing how to hide your sources",
    "Science without religion is lame, religion without science is blind",
    "Everything that is really great and inspiring is created by" +
       "the individual who can labor in freedom"
  };
  ArrayList list = new ArrayList(Arrays.asList(quotes));
  Random r = new Random();
  int x = r.nextInt(list.size());
  String saying = (String)list.get(x);
  saying = saying + " -- Albert Einstein";
  pageContext.setAttribute("saying", saying);
%>

<html>
  <head>
      <title>JBoss Notebook Chapter 2 Demo 1</title>
  </head>
  <body>
    <br>
    <c:set var="sessionCount" scope="session"
           value="${sessionCount + 1}" />
    <c:set var="applicationCount" scope="application"
           value="${applicationCount + 1}" />
    <h1>
        <font color="#1230cb">The Great Albert Einstein Quote Machine</font>
    </h1>
```

Chapter 2: Deploying an Application on JBoss

```
<h3>
    <spacer size="32" type="horizontal">
    <font color="#a6a6a6">
        ${saying}
    </font>
</h3>
<br><br>
You've visited this application ${sessionCount}
times in this session
<br>
and the application has been visited ${applicationCount}
times by you and others.
</body>
</html>
```

We've made use of JSTL tags here. JBoss doesn't provide a JSTL implementation, so we had to include one with the application.

The application displays a random quotation from an array of Einstein's quotes. The code to select the quote is a JSP scriptlet at the top of the page. In a larger application, we'd prefer that this code not be in the JSP. But for illustrative purposes, it's just fine. The application also manages a hit counter. That will be useful to us later, to detect when the application has been redeployed.

The static JSP and HTML files live in the top directory of the WAR file, so our *quote.jsp* file will go at the top of the directory structure in the *quotes* directory.

The next file, *web.xml*, goes into the *WEB-INF* directory. The *web.xml* file describes the web application and how the web container will deploy the application.

```
<?xml version="1.0" ?>
<web-app xmlns="http://java.sun.com/xml/ns/j2ee"
    xmlns:xsi="http://www.w3.org/2001/XMLSchema-instance"
    xsi:schemaLocation="http://java.sun.com/xml/ns/j2ee
                        http://java.sun.com/xml/ns/j2ee/web-app_2_4.xsd"
    version="2.4">

    <servlet>
        <servlet-name>QuoteServlet</servlet-name>
        <jsp-file>/quote.jsp</jsp-file>
    </servlet>
    <servlet-mapping>
        <servlet-name>QuoteServlet</servlet-name>
        <url-pattern>/quote</url-pattern>
    </servlet-mapping>
</web-app>
```

Notice that the *quote.jsp* file we looked at before is related to a servlet named QuoteServlet. This is the name of the servlet that the *quote.jsp* file is exposed as. Next you can see the URL pathname that we will use to refer to the servlet when we are in the web browser.

Any dependent JAR files for libraries you might use in your web application tion go in the *lib* directory. The *classes* directory contains the beans or servlets you've created for your application. We have no beans or servlets for our example application. That's it for the WAR file.

Let's look at the Ant build file that creates our WAR file from our sources and libraries. You can see the setup for development sources in Figure 2-2.

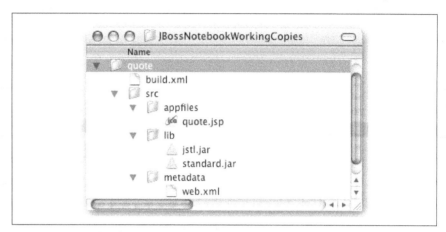

Figure 2-2. Quote source directories

The Ant build file, *build.xml*, pulls together all the stuff for our application, and makes the WAR file. It also has tasks for deploying, undeploying and cleaning.

```
<?xml version="1.0"?>

<!-- Build file for hello_world project for Chapter 2 of JBoss Notebook -->
<project name="Hello World Buildfile" default="main" basedir=".">
    <!-- Standard Properties -->
    <property name="top.dir" value="."/>
    <property name="src.dir" value="${top.dir}/src"/>
    <property name="lib.dir" value="${top.dir}/src/lib"/>
    <property name="jboss.dir" value="/users/samjr/jboss-4.0.2"/>
    <property name="jboss.deploy.dir"
            value="${jboss.dir}/server/default/deploy"/>

    <target name="clean">
        <echo message="In clean"/>
        <delete file="${top.dir}/quote.war"/>
    </target>

    <target name="main">
        <echo message="In main"/>
        <war warfile="quote.war" webxml="${src.dir}/metadata/web.xml">
            <fileset dir="${src.dir}/appfiles"/>
            <lib dir="${lib.dir}"/>
        </war>
```

```
            <antcall target="deploy"/>
    </target>

    <target name="deploy">
            <echo message="In deploy"/>
            <copy file="${top.dir}/quote.war" todir="${jboss.deploy.dir}"/>
    </target>

    <target name="undeploy">
            <echo message="In undeploy"/>
            <delete>
                    <fileset id="quote_wars" dir="${jboss.deploy.dir}"
                        includes="*quote*.war"/>
            </delete>
    </target>

</project>
```

For this *build.xml* file to work for you you'll have to change the jboss.dir property to point to the directory in which you installed JBoss.

Open a terminal window and go to the *quotes* directory. Type ant to kick off the build. This command triggers the default build path, which is specified by the default property in the project tag. In our Ant build file, the default case is to call the main target. Our main target also runs the deploy target, so as soon as the application is packaged up in a WAR file, it is copied over to the server's *deploy* directory.

The most important part of the *build.xml* file for this example is the war tag in the main target. That war tag creates the WAR file we'll deploy by packing up the *web.xml* file, our JSP, and the JSTL libraries that we talked about before.

```
[quote]$ ant
Buildfile: build.xml

main:
     [echo] In main
      [war] Building war: /Users/samjr/JBossNotebookWorkingCopies/quote/
quote.war

deploy:
     [echo] In deploy
     [copy] Copying 1 file to /users/samjr/jboss-4.0.2/server/default/deploy

BUILD SUCCESSFUL
Total time: 4 seconds
```

WARNING

Web applications have to be deployed using the WAR file format in JBoss. There is no easy-to-include web content outside of a WAR file.

You can also set the jboss.dir property from the command line using the -D option to Ant or an Ant properties file, but you'll probably find it more convenient to just edit the build file.

In the terminal window where you have JBoss running, you should see something like this:

```
05:30:14,655 INFO  [Server] JBoss (MX MicroKernel) [4.0.2RC1 (build:
CVSTag=JBoss_4_0_2_RC1 date=200503140913)] Started in 53s:894ms
05:30:29,107 INFO  [TomcatDeployer] undeploy, ctxPath=/quote, warUrl=file:/
Users/samjr/jboss-4.0.2/server/default/tmp/deploy/tmp12811quote.war/
05:30:29,273 INFO  [TomcatDeployer] deploy, ctxPath=/quote, warUrl=file:/
Users/samjr/jboss-4.0.2/server/default/tmp/deploy/tmp12812quote.war/
```

If you are running JBoss in a clustered environment, you can use the farm service to deploy or undeploy an application across the entire cluster.

The output shows that we deployed the application right after the server started. There aren't any stack traces (a good sign), and the word *deploy* appears right after *[TomcatDeployer]*. If there is already a WAR file of the same name, JBoss undeploys it and redeploys the new version of your application. In this example, we had our application deployed already. When we rebuilt and redeployed the application, JBoss took care of getting the old version out and putting the new version in. This is called *hot deployment*. This feature allows you to upgrade your application without taking the server offline.

What just happened?

You ran the build script, which created a WAR file with *quote.jsp*, two libraries (*jstl.jar* and *standard.jar*), and the *web.xml* file in it. Additionally, the build script copied the WAR file over to the *deploy* directory of the server's `default` configuration.

This behavior is controlled by the deployment scanner service. Like all services, it is completely configurable. With it, you can control where JBoss looks for applications and how frequently it checks for updates.

Then you saw in the window where you see the basic logging output from the server that the web application did indeed deploy. You also saw how hot deployment allows you to redeploy an application in a live server.

If you didn't have a build script that copied the WAR file over to the *deploy* directory, you could do it by hand and you would still see the application being deployed in the server's terminal window. The build script did nothing besides copy the WAR file to the deployment directory. No special configuration was needed. JBoss just sensed that a new file was there to be deployed, scanned it to find the deployment descriptor, and then did its thing. Nice and easy.

What about...

...deployment errors?

If you had an error, you'd see it in the console log. This is usually accompanied by a stack trace or other contextual information to give you an idea of what the problem is. If you don't see any errors, you can be fairly certain the application deployed successfully. As an example, we tried to deploy a WAR file with an invalid *web.xml* file. This caused the following error message:

```
17:48:16,033 ERROR [XmlFileLoader] Invalid XML: file=file:/private/tmp/
jboss-4.0.2/server/default/tmp/deploy/tmp2254quote.war//WEB-INF/web.xml@1:2
…
17:48:17,464 ERROR [ContextConfig] Occurred at line 2 column 1
17:48:17,464 ERROR [ContextConfig] Marking this application unavailable due
to previous error(s)
17:48:17,464 ERROR [StandardContext] Error getConfigured
17:48:17,469 ERROR [StandardContext] Context startup failed due to previous
errors17:48:17,503 ERROR [WebModule] Starting failed jboss.web.deployment:
id=-110422429,war=quote.war
org.jboss.deployment.DeploymentException: URL file:/private/tmp/jboss-4.0.2/
server/default/tmp/deploy/tmp2254quote.war/ deployment failed
…
17:48:17,522 WARN  [ServiceController] Problem starting service jboss.web.
deployment:id=-110422429,war=quote.war
org.jboss.deployment.DeploymentException: URL file:/private/tmp/jboss-4.0.2/
server/default/tmp/deploy/tmp2254quote.war/ deployment failed
```

The output is much more verbose than what we've shown here, but the error messages give you a very clear picture of what is wrong.

Use the tail command on the log files to monitor what is being logged.

What about getting more detailed information about the deployment process?

The server log file, *server/default/logs/server.log*, contains more detailed logging information about the deployment process. If you are trying to track down a non-critical deployment error, the information there can be very helpful. Here's an example:

```
2005-03-21 05:30:29,178 DEBUG [org.jboss.deployment.MainDeployer] Starting
deployment of package: file:/Users/samjr/jboss-4.0.2/server/default/deploy/
quote.war
2005-03-21 05:30:29,179 DEBUG [org.jboss.deployment.MainDeployer] Starting
deployment (init step) of package at: file:/Users/samjr/jboss-4.0.2/server/
default/deploy/quote.war
2005-03-21 05:30:29,179 DEBUG [org.jboss.deployment.MainDeployer] Copying
file:/Users/samjr/jboss-4.0.2/server/default/deploy/quote.war -> /Users/
samjr/jboss-4.0.2/server/default/tmp/deploy/tmp12812quote.war
2005-03-21 05:30:29,190 DEBUG [org.jboss.deployment.MainDeployer] using
deployer org.jboss.web.tomcat.tc5.Tomcat5@54b5d4
2005-03-21 05:30:29,190 DEBUG [org.jboss.web.tomcat.tc5.Tomcat5] Begin init
2005-03-21 05:30:29,195 DEBUG [org.jboss.web.tomcat.tc5.Tomcat5] Unpacking
war to: /Users/samjr/jboss-4.0.2/server/default/tmp/deploy/tmp12812quote-
exp.war
2005-03-21 05:30:29,251 DEBUG [org.jboss.web.tomcat.tc5.Tomcat5] Replaced
war with unpacked contents

[more lines of info removed for brevity]

] Initialized: {WebApplication: /Users/samjr/jboss-4.0.2/server/default/tmp/
deploy/tmp12812quote.war/, URL: file:/Users/samjr/jboss-4.0.2/server/
```

```
default/tmp/deploy/tmp12812quote.war/, classLoader: java.net.
FactoryURLClassLoader@dcf865:14481509} jboss.web:
J2EEApplication=none,J2EEServer=none,j2eeType=WebModule,name=//localhost/
quote
2005-03-21 05:30:29,579 DEBUG [org.jboss.web.WebModule] Started jboss.web.
deployment:id=-381072946,war=quote.war
2005-03-21 05:30:29,579 DEBUG [org.jboss.system.ServiceController] Starting
dependent components for: jboss.web.deployment:id=-381072946,war=quote.war
dependent components: [ ]
2005-03-21 05:30:29,579 DEBUG [org.jboss.webservice.ServiceDeployer]
handleNotification: org.jboss.deployment.SubDeployer.start,quote.war
2005-03-21 05:30:29,600 DEBUG [org.jboss.deployment.MainDeployer] End
deployment start on package: quote.war
2005-03-21 05:30:29,600 DEBUG [org.jboss.deployment.MainDeployer] Deployed
package: file:/Users/samjr/jboss-4.0.2/server/default/deploy/quote.war
```

You can see that the WAR file is unpacked, and the unpacked version replaces the packed version, etc. We took out a lot to fit it in the book, but needless to say there is a lot to see and you should go look around.

Running the Application

To run the application, first we need to know what the URL is to access the application. You can figure this out by looking at the *web.xml* and *build.xml* files. The path to use in the URL is based on the WAR file's name and the url-pattern from the servlet-mapping section in the *web.xml* file. In our case the WAR file is named *quote.war* and the servlet mapping is quote. This gives us the path */quote/quote*, which we put together with the host and port portion of a URL.

How do I do that?

Open your web browser and go to *http://localhost:8080/quote/quote*. You should see something like Figure 2-3.

Leave the web browser open, as you'll probably want to use it in the next lab. You might want to click the browser's refresh button to see the counts on the page go up. After you've done that a few times, do another build. Once that build is done and deployed, click the browser's refresh button a few more times. Now you should see that the counts are different (see Figure 2-4). The application count gets reset each time the servlet is reloaded, which happens whenever you deploy the application. However, the session state doesn't get reset. So, the server is maintaining state; and you're not losing it when you do a redeploy. Hot deploy makes this possible.

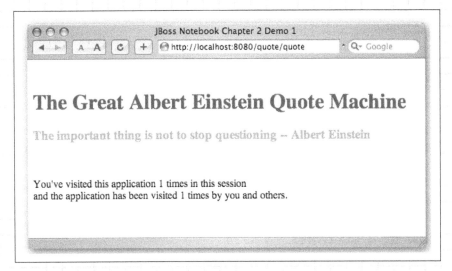

Figure 2-3. Einstein quote server

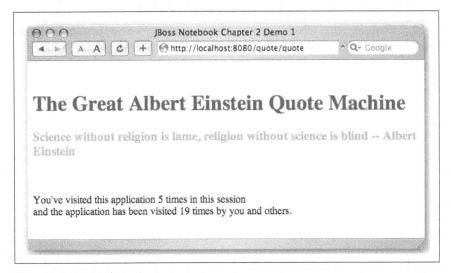

Figure 2-4. Count changes

What just happened?

When you went to the URL for the application, the application compiled and created a servlet based on what is specified in the servlet section of the *web.xml* file. Then JBoss deployed that servlet and created a mapping based on the servlet-mapping section of the *web.xml* file. Again, the URL is based on the WAR filename created by the build (look in *build.xml*) and the URL pattern mapping in the *web.xml* file.

You also got to see hot deploy in action. Plus, you got a few tidbits of advice from the great Einstein himself.

Modifying the Deployed Application

Hot deployment allows you to rapidly deploy an application in JBoss by simply placing the application in the *deploy* directory. JBoss quickly sees the application and deploys it, but ideally you would like to be able to make changes to a live application without deployment delays, no matter how small.

How do I do that?

JBoss unpacks those pesky J2EE archives into the *tmp/deploy* directory. The names are slightly mangled, but you should see a directory whose name ends in *quote.war*. This directory contains the fully expanded contents of *quote.war*. Each time you redeploy your application JBoss removes the current temporary directory and replaces it with one of a slightly different name.

If you need to check which version of your application is deployed, check the tmp/deploy directory. Whatever you see there is what JBoss currently has deployed.

WARNING

You will see a temporary copy of everything you see in the *lib* and *deploy* directories. JBoss doesn't keep an open handle on any of the files in those directories. This is very important if your operating system keeps a lock on files while they are being read.

If you edit the *quote.jsp* file in the expanded *quote.war* directory, you will see the changes reflected the next time you access the application. That's all you have to do to test out a minor change to a live web application.

You can update JSPs and static web content, but unfortunately you can't update the deployment descriptors. You'll have to redeploy the entire application to pick up a change to them.

What about...

...the compiled JSPs?

If you run into a problem where you need to see the compiled JSPs, look in the *work/jboss.web/localhost/* directory. The generated Java code is available in a subdirectory named after the context the web application serves.

Exploding Deployments

We're sure you can see the power of being able to access the temporary directory JBoss uses to hold expanded archives. If you find yourself wanting to use this feature a lot, JBoss supports the notion of an exploded deployment. Instead of deploying your application in its normal archived form, you can deploy it as a fully expanded directory and save JBoss the trouble of copying it out to the temporary directory.

How do I do that?

The exploded WAR directory has the exact same structure as a regular WAR file. Our build file could easily be modified to build to a WAR directory, but since we have a WAR file already made, we'll just use that.

From the *deploy* directory, we'll expand *quote.war* into a new WAR directory using the jar command:

```
[deploy]$ mkdir quote2.war
[deploy]$ cd quote2.war/
[quote2.war]$ jar xvf ../quote.war
  created: META-INF/
extracted: META-INF/MANIFEST.MF
extracted: quote.jsp
  created: WEB-INF/
  created: WEB-INF/lib/
extracted: WEB-INF/lib/jstl.jar
extracted: WEB-INF/lib/standard.jar
extracted: WEB-INF/web.xml
[quote2.war]$ ls
META-INF        WEB-INF         quote.jsp
```

You won't find a copy of the application in tmp/deploy when you deploy an exploded archive. It's just not needed.

If you check the console log, you'll see the application has been deployed. Since the new application is deployed as *quote2.war*, you'll access it at a slightly different URL than before: *http://localhost:8080/quote2/quote*.

You can edit *quote.jsp* in the live application, just as you did in the last lab. What is more interesting is that you can edit the deployment descriptors now. When JBoss detects a change to the *web.xml* file, it will redeploy the whole application. Try adding an additional servlet mapping for *quote.jsp* and watch the application redeploy.

What just happened?

We discovered how to deploy applications on JBoss in exploded form. This isn't limited to WAR files. Any J2EE archive can be deployed in exploded form. A nested archive, such as a WAR file inside of an EAR file, for

Nesting archives is called Russian Doll Packaging in JBoss. JBoss supports arbitrary nesting of archives. Any package type can contain any other. If you want an EAR file inside of another EAR file, for example, JBoss is happy to oblige.

example, can be deployed as nested directories. JBoss will always monitor the topmost J2EE deployment descriptor (`application.xml`, in the case of the EAR file example) to know when to redeploy the application.

Viewing the Application on the Management Console

Now that we've deployed the application and run it, let's see what it looks like in the JBoss Console. We'll take just a quick look at the console for now, but later in the book we will cover it in much more depth.

How do I do that?

To see the application in the JBoss Console, you need to open your web browser and go to *http://localhost:8080/web-console/*. You'll see a screen like Figure 2-5.

Figure 2-5. Web console open to quote.war

You can see *quote.war* under the JBoss server. You can see that it has `QuoteServlet` in it, which is what we told it to create from the *quote.jsp* file in *web.xml*. If you choose `QuoteServlet`, you will see servlet statistics about it, including the number of times it has been invoked (see Figure 2-6).

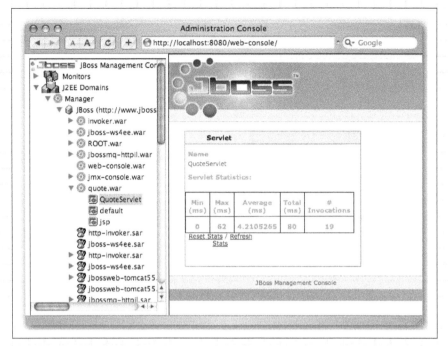

Figure 2-6. Servlet statistics

If you have not closed your web browser, you can reload the application at *http://localhost:8080/quote/quote* and then click QuoteServlet again to cause the web console application to refresh, at which point you should see the "# Invocations" count go up (see Figure 2-7).

What just happened?

You just saw the JBoss web console and your application deployed onto the server. You also saw that when you ran your application again, the web console could show you those changes. We will spend quite a bit more time on the web console later in the book, but for now we just wanted to give you a quick view of it and show you the possibilities.

Uninstalling the Application

Now, like all good things, our application's time in the limelight has to come to an end. It has served its purpose of entertaining and informing us and now we are ready to undeploy it. Let's see how to do that on JBoss.

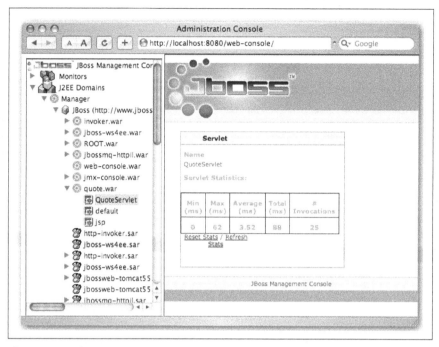

Figure 2-7. Going up, up, up

How do I do that?

If you deploy an application by placing it into the *deploy* directory, it stands to reason that undeploying should happen when you remove it from the *deploy* directory. Sure enough, that holds true. If you delete the *quote.war* file, JBoss notices this change and undeploys the application. You should get a notice such as this in the log:

```
08:56:13,629 INFO  [TomcatDeployer] undeploy, ctxPath=/quote, warUrl=file:/
Users/samjr/jboss-4.0.2/server/default/tmp/deploy/tmp12813quote.war/
```

We've also provided an undeploy target that accomplishes this. As you can see, the build file is just deleting the file from the *deploy* directory:

```
[quote]$ ant undeploy
Buildfile: build.xml

undeploy:
     [echo] In undeploy
   [delete] Deleting 1 files from /users/samjr/jboss-4.0.2/server/default/
deploy

BUILD SUCCESSFUL
```

And that's it; the application is gone! This was just a simple web application; we'll move on to a more complete J2EE application in the next chapter.

Creating a Complete Application

We're going to take a big step, from a simple web application to a complete J2EE application with both a web and an EJB component. J2EE has a reputation for being complex and requiring a lot of configuration to make it work. That reputation is not entirely undeserved, but it is possible to work with J2EE and avoid much of the complexity.

We'll use two tools to do this. The first is XDoclet. XDoclet is a code-generation tool that allows a developer to work with a single bean class instead of worrying about the myriad related classes that need to be developed. This model resembles the simplified EJB development model that will be introduced in EJB3, except that the metadata is stored in untyped Javadoc-style comments rather than proper language-level metadata. XDoclet also manages the generation of both J2EE and application server-specific deployment descriptors.

The second tool is JBoss itself. JBoss is extremely developer friendly in that you can quickly deploy an application on JBoss without worrying about database integration, security configuration, or any of the other details that can slow down your application development. That is exactly the approach we will take here. We won't ignore those topics forever, but we will skip over them initially and let JBoss fill in the blanks.

The application we will build is a web-based ToDo list manager. Users can log into the application and manage a personal list of items they are working on. The web application is a JavaServer Faces application that talks to Enterprise JavaBeans™ on the back end. Although it is fairly simple structurally, few J2EE applications get any more complicated than this.

The source code for the application is in the *todo* directory of the example code. You'll want to keep the application code within reach as we go through the example because we won't be focusing on the code. We will

We are focusing on J2EE applications. But don't think that JBoss is just a J2EE server. There is much more: AOP, Hibernate and MBeans, to name just a few.

focus on what it takes to make an application run in JBoss. To that end, the actual code is little more than an application detail. You won't need to be overly concerned about the details. You can imagine any J2EE application that you have worked on in its place.

But that's enough talk. Let's get the application going.

Building the EJB Tier

The ToDo application looks like any other J2EE application. It consists of an EJB JAR file that contains the EJBs, and a WAR file that provides the web application code. Both of these are wrapped up in an EAR file that comprises the entire enterprise application. Since the web tier depends on the EJB tier, we'll start there.

How do I do that?

The EJB tier consists of two local CMP entity beans, TaskBean and CommentBean, and one local session bean, TaskMasterBean. You can find the source code for all the beans in the *src/com/oreilly/jbossnotebook/todo/ejb* directory.

Notice that there are only three source files for the three enterprise beans, instead of the dozen or so you might normally expect to write. XDoclet will do the heavy lifting and generate all the required J2EE interfaces, as well as a host of other supporting classes.

See the build.xml file for the taskdef operations required to load the XDoclet tasks.

TIP

XDoclet isn't just a great tool for developing EJB applications. It's used to develop the JBoss server itself. You'll find XDoclet attributes throughout the JBoss code tree.

The *build.xml* file contains the ejbdoclet target, which is responsible for invoking the XDoclet-provided ejbdoclet task. This code-generation step needs to take place right before the compile step.

```
<target name="ejbdoclet" depends="init">
    <mkdir dir="dd/ejb" />

    <ejbdoclet destdir="${gen.src.dir}" ejbSpec="2.1">
        <fileset dir="${src.dir}">
            <include name="**/*Bean.java"/>
        </fileset>

        <deploymentdescriptor destdir="dd/ejb"/>
```

```
            <homeinterface/>
            <remoteinterface/>
            <localinterface/>
            <localhomeinterface/>

            <utilobject includeGUID="true" cacheHomes="true" />
            <valueobject pattern="{0}"/>
            <entitycmp/>
            <session/>
        </ejbdoclet>
    </target>
```

If would be nice if we didn't need to generate so many classes, but all things considered, it isn't so bad when you are using XDoclet.

Each subtask inside the `ejbdoclet` task represents one unique code-generation task XDoclet provides. We will be generating nine different types of classes.

As an example of what XDoclet does, take a look at one of the entity beans. Notice in Example 3-1 that all the metadata and bean configuration are done using special tags inside of Javadoc comments.

Example 3-1. The TaskBean entity bean

```java
package com.oreilly.jbossnotebook.todo.ejb;

import java.util.Date;
import java.util.Set;

import javax.ejb.CreateException;
import javax.ejb.EntityBean;


/**
 * Entity bean representing a blog entry.
 *
 * @ejb.bean name="Task"
 *           type="CMP"
 *           cmp-version="2.x"
 *           view-type="local"
 *           primkey-field="id"
 *
 * @ejb.finder signature="java.util.Collection findAll( )"
 *           query="SELECT OBJECT(t) FROM Task AS t"
 *
 * @ejb.finder
 *    signature="java.util.Collection findTasksForUser(java.lang.String user)"
 *    query="SELECT OBJECT(t) FROM Task AS t WHERE t.user = ?1"
 *
 * @ejb.value-object name="Task"
 */
public abstract class TaskBean
    implements EntityBean
{
```

The XDoclet attributes closely resemble the annotations model that will be used in EJB3.

Example 3-1. The TaskBean entity bean (continued)

```
    /** @ejb.create-method */
    public String ejbCreate(String user, String name)
        throws CreateException
    {
...
    }

    public void ejbPostCreate(String name, String user)
        throws CreateException
    {
    }
    /**
     * @ejb.pk-field
     * @ejb.persistence
     * @ejb.interface-method
     */
    public abstract String getId( );
    public abstract void setId(String id);

    /**
     * @ejb.persistence
     * @ejb.interface-method
     */
    public abstract String getName( );
    /** @ejb.interface-method */
    public abstract void setName(String name);

    /**
     * @ejb.persistence
     * @ejb.interface-method
     */
    public abstract String getUser( );

    /** @ejb.interface-method */
    public abstract void setUser(String topic);

    /**
     * @ejb.persistence
     * @ejb.interface-method
     */
    public abstract Date getStartedDate( );
    /** @ejb.interface-method */
    public abstract void setStartedDate(Date date);

    /**
     * @ejb.persistence
     * @ejb.interface-method
     */
    public abstract Date getCompletedDate( );
    /** @ejb.interface-method */
    public abstract void setCompletedDate(Date date);
    /**
```

Container-managed persistence is much simpler when you don't have to worry about the deployment descriptor.

Example 3-1. *The TaskBean entity bean (continued)*

```
 * @ejb.interface-method
 *
 * @ejb.relation name="task-comment"
 *               role-name="task-has-comments"
 * @ejb.value-object
 *       aggregate="com.oreilly.jbossnotebook.todo.ejb.Comment"
 *       aggregate-name="Comment"
 *       members="com.oreilly.jbossnotebook.todo.ejb.CommentLocal"
 *       members-name="Comments"
 *       relation="external"
 *       type="java.util.Set"
 *
 */
public abstract Set getComments( );

/** @ejb.interface-method */
public abstract void setComments(Set comments);

/** @ejb.interface-method */
public abstract Task getTask( );
/** @ejb.interface-method */
public abstract void setTask(Task task);
}
```

Everything related to this bean is declared in the bean class. The @ejb.create-method and @ejb.finder attributes tell XDoclet how to generate the local home interface. Example 3-2 shows the generated interface.

Example 3-2. *The generated local home interface*

```
package com.oreilly.jbossnotebook.todo.ejb;

/**
 * Local home interface for Task.
 */
public interface TaskLocalHome
   extends javax.ejb.EJBLocalHome
{
   public static final String COMP_NAME="java:comp/env/ejb/TaskLocal";
   public static final String JNDI_NAME="TaskLocal";

   public com.oreilly.jbossnotebook.todo.ejb.TaskLocal
         create(java.lang.String user , java.lang.String name)
      throws javax.ejb.CreateException;

   public java.util.Collection findAll( )
      throws javax.ejb.FinderException;

   public java.util.Collection findTasksForUser(java.lang.String user)
      throws javax.ejb.FinderException;
```

The localhomeinterface subtask generates local home interfaces.

The localinterface subtask generates local interfaces.

Example 3-2. The generated local home interface (continued)

```
    public com.oreilly.jbossnotebook.todo.ejb.TaskLocal
        findByPrimaryKey(java.lang.String pk)
      throws javax.ejb.FinderException;
}
```

The local interface is based on the signatures of methods marked with @ejb.interface. Example 3-3 shows the generated local interface.

Example 3-3. The generated local interface

```
package com.oreilly.jbossnotebook.todo.ejb;

/**
 * Local interface for Task.
 */
public interface TaskLocal
   extends javax.ejb.EJBLocalObject
{
    public java.lang.String getId( );
    public java.lang.String getName( );
    public void setName(java.lang.String name);
    public java.lang.String getUser( );
    public void setUser(java.lang.String topic);
    public java.util.Date getStartedDate( );
    public void setStartedDate(java.util.Date date);
    public java.util.Date getCompletedDate( );
    public void setCompletedDate(java.util.Date date);
    public java.util.Set getComments( );
    public void setComments(java.util.Set comments);
    public com.oreilly.jbossnotebook.todo.ejb.Task getTask( );
    public void setTask(com.oreilly.jbossnotebook.todo.ejb.Task task);
}
```

The valueobject subtask generates the value objects.

Entity beans aren't meant to be passed all the way up the web tier. We need to shuttle the entity values in and out through a value object. The @ejb.value-object attributes determine which fields and relations should be represented on the value object that the application code will use. Example 3-4 shows the generated task value object.

Example 3-4. The generated value object

```
package com.oreilly.jbossnotebook.todo.ejb;

/**
 * Value object for Task.
 *
 */
public class Task
   extends java.lang.Object
   implements java.io.Serializable
{
```

Example 3-4. The generated value object (continued)

```
// [… private instance variables …]

public Task( ) {}

public Task(java.lang.String id,
            java.lang.String name,java.lang.String user,
            java.util.Date startedDate,
            java.util.Date completedDate)
{… }

public Task( Task otherValue ) { … }

public java.lang.String getPrimaryKey( ) { … }
public void setPrimaryKey( java.lang.String pk ) { … }

public java.lang.String getId( ) { … }
public void setId(java.lang.String id) { … }
public boolean idHasBeenSet( ) { … }

public java.lang.String getName( ) { … }
public void setName(java.lang.String name) { … }
public boolean nameHasBeenSet( ) { … }

public java.lang.String getUser( ) { … }
public void setUser(java.lang.String user) { … }
public boolean userHasBeenSet( ) { … }

public java.util.Date getStartedDate( ) { … }
public void setStartedDate(java.util.Date startedDate) { … }
public boolean startedDateHasBeenSet( ) { … }

public java.util.Date getCompletedDate( ) {… }
public void setCompletedDate( java.util.Date completedDate ) {… }
public boolean completedDateHasBeenSet( ) {… }

public java.util.Set getAddedComments( ) { return addedComments; }
public java.util.Set getOnceAddedComments( ) { return onceAddedComments; }
public java.util.Set getRemovedComments( ) { return removedComments; }
public java.util.Set getUpdatedComments( ) { return updatedComments; }
public void setAddedComments(java.util.Set addedComments) { … }
public void setOnceAddedComments(java.util.Set onceAddedComments) { … }
public void setRemovedComments(java.util.Set removedComments) { … }
public void setUpdatedComments(java.util.Set updatedComments) { … }

public com.oreilly.jbossnotebook.todo.ejb.Comment[ ] getComments( ) { … }
public void setComments(com.oreilly.jbossnotebook.todo.ejb.Comment[ ] Comments) {… }
public void clearComments( ) { … }

public void addComment(com.oreilly.jbossnotebook.todo.ejb.Comment added) {… }
public void removeComment(com.oreilly.jbossnotebook.todo.ejb.Comment removed) {… }
public void updateComment(com.oreilly.jbossnotebook.todo.ejb.Comment updated) {… }
public void cleanComment( ) {… }
```

Dirty checks and relation management in value objects can get very tricky. Aren't you glad you don't need to write these methods?

Methods such as toString( ), equals( ), and hashCode( ) are difficult to keep in sync with changes to the entity bean. XDoclet ensures that these methods are always current.

Example 3-4. The generated value object (continued)

```
    public void copyCommentsFrom(com.oreilly.jbossnotebook.todo.ejb.Task from) { … }
    public String toString() { … }
    protected boolean hasIdentity() { … }
    public boolean equals(Object other) { … }
    public boolean isIdentical(Object other) { … }
    public int hashCode() { … }
}
```

Where do the value object instances get created? XDoclet can generate a subclass of our bean that provides the methods to create and consume the value objects, as well as the default implementations of the entity bean lifecycle methods. The CMP subclass helper gets very little attention, but it is one of the more valuable XDoclet tasks. Managing value objects is hard work. Example 3-5 shows the generated CMP subclass.

Example 3-5. The generated CMP subclass

```
package com.oreilly.jbossnotebook.todo.ejb;

/**
 * CMP layer for Task.
 */
public abstract class TaskCMP
    extends com.oreilly.jbossnotebook.todo.ejb.TaskBean
    implements javax.ejb.EntityBean
{
```

The entitycmp task generates the CMP subclass.

```
    public void ejbLoad() { }
    public void ejbStore() { }
    public void ejbActivate() { }
    public void ejbPassivate() {… }
    public void setEntityContext(javax.ejb.EntityContext ctx) { }
    public void unsetEntityContext() { }
    public void ejbRemove()
        throws javax.ejb.RemoveException
    {}
```

setTask( ) and setTask( ) perform the actual work of creating and consuming the value objects.

```
    /* Value Objects BEGIN */

    public void addComments(com.oreilly.jbossnotebook.todo.ejb.Comment added)
        throws javax.ejb.FinderException
    {… }

    public void removeComments(com.oreilly.jbossnotebook.todo.ejb.Comment removed)
        throws javax.ejb.RemoveException
    {… }

    private com.oreilly.jbossnotebook.todo.ejb.Task Task = null;

    public com.oreilly.jbossnotebook.todo.ejb.Task getTask()
    {… }
```

Example 3-5. The generated CMP subclass (continued)

```
    public void setTask(com.oreilly.jbossnotebook.todo.ejb.Task valueHolder)
    {… }

    /* Value Objects END */

    public abstract java.lang.String getId( ) ;
    public abstract void setId( java.lang.String id ) ;
    public abstract java.lang.String getName( ) ;
    public abstract void setName( java.lang.String name ) ;
    public abstract java.lang.String getUser( ) ;
    public abstract void setUser( java.lang.String user ) ;
    public abstract java.util.Date getStartedDate( ) ;
    public abstract void setStartedDate( java.util.Date startedDate ) ;
    public abstract java.util.Date getCompletedDate( ) ;
    public abstract void setCompletedDate( java.util.Date completedDate ) ;
}
```

Finally, XDoclet generates a helpful utility class which provides convenience methods for looking up the local home interface from JNDI and for the generation of UUIDs that can be used as a surrogate key in the database. Example 3-6 shows the generated TaskUtil class, with the long UUID code omitted.

The utilobject subtask generates the bean helper utility class.

Example 3-6. The generated EJB helper class

```
package com.oreilly.jbossnotebook.todo.ejb;

/**
 * Utility class for Task.
 */
public class TaskUtil
{
    /** Cached local home (EJBLocalHome). Uses lazy loading to obtain
     * its value (loaded by getLocalHome( ) methods).
     */
    private static com.oreilly.jbossnotebook.todo.ejb.TaskLocalHome
                cachedLocalHome = null;

    private static Object lookupHome(java.util.Hashtable environment,
                                 String jndiName, Class narrowTo)
        throws javax.naming.NamingException
    {… }

    // UUID code deleted
}
```

The bean sets the JNDI name to look up from the generated local home object.

We've only shown the code for TaskBean, but similar code is generated for CommentBean and TaskMasterBean. That is a lot of code—1,403 lines over 14 files, according to the wc command:

```
[ejb]$ wc -l *
    202 Comment.java
     96 CommentCMP.java
     31 CommentLocal.java
     24 CommentLocalHome.java
    116 CommentUtil.java
    387 Task.java
    169 TaskCMP.java
     39 TaskLocal.java
     27 TaskLocalHome.java
     25 TaskMasterLocal.java
     18 TaskMasterLocalHome.java
     37 TaskMasterSession.java
    116 TaskMasterUtil.java
    116 TaskUtil.java
   1403 total
```

We have one more task for XDoclet. XDoclet will generate *ejb-jar.xml* for us. Since the deployment descriptor is so standard, we won't show it here. Just keep in mind that XDoclet has generated the information for all the persistent fields and relationships, the queries, and all the security and transaction declarations. Where we haven't specified the details in our class, XDoclet assumes reasonable defaults.

With our entire EJB tier complete, we need to compile the code and place it, along with the deployment descriptor, into an EJB JAR file:

```
[todo]$ jar tf build/jars/todo.jar
META-INF/
META-INF/MANIFEST.MF
META-INF/ejb-jar.xml
com/
com/oreilly/
com/oreilly/jbossnotebook/
com/oreilly/jbossnotebook/todo/
com/oreilly/jbossnotebook/todo/ejb/
com/oreilly/jbossnotebook/todo/ejb/Comment.class
com/oreilly/jbossnotebook/todo/ejb/CommentBean.class
com/oreilly/jbossnotebook/todo/ejb/CommentCMP.class
com/oreilly/jbossnotebook/todo/ejb/CommentLocal.class
com/oreilly/jbossnotebook/todo/ejb/CommentLocalHome.class
com/oreilly/jbossnotebook/todo/ejb/CommentUtil.class
com/oreilly/jbossnotebook/todo/ejb/Task.class
com/oreilly/jbossnotebook/todo/ejb/TaskBean.class
com/oreilly/jbossnotebook/todo/ejb/TaskCMP.class
com/oreilly/jbossnotebook/todo/ejb/TaskLocal.class
com/oreilly/jbossnotebook/todo/ejb/TaskLocalHome.class
com/oreilly/jbossnotebook/todo/ejb/TaskMasterBean.class
com/oreilly/jbossnotebook/todo/ejb/TaskMasterLocal.class
com/oreilly/jbossnotebook/todo/ejb/TaskMasterLocalHome.class
com/oreilly/jbossnotebook/todo/ejb/TaskMasterSession.class
com/oreilly/jbossnotebook/todo/ejb/TaskMasterUtil.class
com/oreilly/jbossnotebook/todo/ejb/TaskUtil.class
```

What just happened?

We generated a complete EJB application, having only written just a little over 300 lines of code:

```
[ejb]$ wc -l *
    87 CommentBean.java
   117 TaskBean.java
   129 TaskMasterBean.java
   333 total
```

It's easy to see why J2EE developers who don't use a tool such as XDoclet can be frustrated by the amount of code they have to write. While we won't claim to be happy that we have to generate code, it is great to have a tool such as XDoclet that can take care of the complexity.

Most of the code we wrote was actually just metadata.

What about...

...the JBoss deployment descriptors?

XDoclet does have support for generating JBoss deployment descriptors, but so far the application hasn't required any JBoss-specific configuration. That's because the defaults in JBoss make sense for development purposes. We'll explore many of the JBoss customizations in later chapters.

Using XDoclet to Build the Web Tier

The web tier of the application builds on the EJB tier. It provides a simple web interface for a user to manage ToDo items. The application uses JavaServer Faces as the controller. The application needs to provide a few simple backing beans to provide an interface to our back-end EJBs and the JSP pages that make up the view. The JSPs are very standard, so we won't look at them in detail. Instead, we'll look at how we are building and deploying the web tier.

The deployment-descriptor subtask generates the web.xml file.

How do I do that?

Once again, XDoclet will come to our aid to make sure we can get the application up and running as fast as possible. While XDoclet isn't quite the hero on the web tier that it is on the EJB tier, it will help us to generate a good deployment descriptor. The webdoclet task invokes XDoclet for us:

```
<target name="webdoclet" depends="init">
    <mkdir dir="dd/web" />
    <webdoclet destdir="${gen.src.dir}" mergedir="${merge.dir}">
        <fileset dir="${src.dir}">
```

```
                            <include name="**/*Servlet.java"/>
                            <include name="**/*Filter.java"/>
                        </fileset>

                        <deploymentdescriptor servletspec="2.4"
                                              destdir="dd/web"
                                              distributable="false"/>
                    </webdoclet>
                </target>
```

Think of merge files as metadata that isn't associated with any particular Java class.

In the ToDo application, we primarily make use of XDoclet *merge files* to break up the individual configurable elements. Merge files are small code or deployment descriptor fragments that can be inserted into the generated document. The merge files are loaded from the *merge* directory.

The *servlet.xml* file provides the servlet definition for the JSF controller servlet:

```
<servlet>
    <servlet-name>Faces Servlet</servlet-name>
    <servlet-class>javax.faces.webapp.FacesServlet</servlet-class>
    <load-on-startup>1</load-on-startup>
</servlet>
```

The *servlet-mapping.xml* file maps all `.faces` resources to the faces servlet:

```
<servlet-mapping>
    <servlet-name>Faces Servlet</servlet-name>
    <url-pattern>*.faces</url-pattern>
</servlet-mapping>
```

The *web-security.xml* file declares that the application should require users to log in and be assigned the Users role to access the application:

```
<security-constraint>
    <web-resource-collection>
        <web-resource-name>AllFiles</web-resource-name>
        <url-pattern>/*</url-pattern>
        <http-method>GET</http-method>
        <http-method>POST</http-method>
    </web-resource-collection>
    <auth-constraint>
        <role-name>User</role-name>
    </auth-constraint>
</security-constraint>
```

JBoss doesn't care if you declare security roles, but it is good to declare roles for portability.

```
<login-config>
    <auth-method>BASIC</auth-method>
    <realm-name>ToDo Application</realm-name>
</login-config>
```

The *web-sec-roles.xml* file declares that the User role exists:

```
<security-role>
    <role-name>User</role-name>
</security-role>
```

And finally, the *web-ejbrefs-local.xml* file provides a link to the TaskMaster session bean. The backing beans communicate with the EJB tier through the session bean façade.

```
<ejb-local-ref>
    <ejb-ref-name>ejb/TaskMasterLocal</ejb-ref-name>
    <ejb-ref-type>Session</ejb-ref-type>
    <local-home></local-home>
    <local></local>
    <ejb-link>TaskMaster</ejb-link>
</ejb-local-ref>
```

The code for the backing beans is in the *src/com/oreilly/jbossnotebook/ servlet* directory, and the JSPs are in the web directory. The web directory also contains a few additional configuration files the application needs. The most important one is the *faces-config.xml* file used by Java-Server Faces to determine the behavior of the application controller.

When you build the application, the web application is put into todo.war:

```
[todo]$ jar tf build/jars/todo.war
META-INF/
META-INF/MANIFEST.MF
WEB-INF/
WEB-INF/lib/
WEB-INF/lib/commons-beanutils.jar
WEB-INF/lib/commons-collections.jar
WEB-INF/lib/commons-digester.jar
WEB-INF/lib/commons-logging.jar
WEB-INF/lib/jsf-api.jar
WEB-INF/lib/jsf-impl.jar
WEB-INF/lib/jstl.jar
WEB-INF/lib/standard.jar
WEB-INF/classes/
WEB-INF/classes/com/
WEB-INF/classes/com/oreilly/
WEB-INF/classes/com/oreilly/jbossnotebook/
WEB-INF/classes/com/oreilly/jbossnotebook/todo/
WEB-INF/classes/com/oreilly/jbossnotebook/todo/servlet/
WEB-INF/classes/com/oreilly/jbossnotebook/todo/servlet/CreateTaskBean.class
WEB-INF/classes/com/oreilly/jbossnotebook/todo/servlet/DebugBean.class
WEB-INF/classes/com/oreilly/jbossnotebook/todo/servlet/TaskBean.class
WEB-INF/classes/com/oreilly/jbossnotebook/todo/servlet/UserBean.class
WEB-INF/classes/com/oreilly/jbossnotebook/todo/messages.properties
WEB-INF/classes/roles.properties
WEB-INF/classes/users.properties
WEB-INF/faces-config.xml
WEB-INF/web.xml
debug.jsp
front.jsp
list.jsp
style.css
task.jsp
```

With that, we have a complete web application.

What just happened?

Perhaps it is better to start by noting what didn't happen. None of the EJB tier code made its way into the WAR file. There are no EJB interfaces or value objects in the web application. The JBoss classloader gives the web application visibility into the EJB JAR file containing the beans. With JBoss, you don't have any of the packaging hassles you have come to expect from J2EE application servers. There were also no JBoss deployment descriptors. The JBoss defaults are quite reasonable for application development.

Defining Users

Security is the one exception to the rule for which JBoss provides useful defaults. JBoss needs to know how to check the usernames and passwords required to access the application. At first glance it might seem that JBoss could provide a global repository of names and passwords. That would work fine if all that were required were a username and password, but J2EE applications have a notion of role-based authorization. A username needs not only to be valid, but also to be assigned to a specific role named in the deployment descriptor. There's no generic way to map users onto arbitrary roles, so it is necessary to provide that configuration with the application.

How do I do that?

The role name has meaning only to the application. JBoss has no notion of users, administrators, or other such roles.

The default security domain in JBoss looks for user information in properties files inside the application. The first of the properties files is *users.properties*. It provides usernames and passwords. You can find the file in the *web/WEB-INF/classes/* directory:

```
pinky=duh
brain=conquest
```

The property name (on the lefthand side of the equals sign) is the username, and the property value is the password. Go ahead and add your own user to the file.

The other important file is *roles.properties*, which maps users onto roles. We declared the application to require the User role in the *web-security.xml* merge file. We need to make sure that the application users have that role:

```
pinky=User
brain=User
```

Chapter 3: Creating a Complete Application

The property name is the username, and the property value is the role assigned to the user. The ToDo application uses only one role, but if we had more than one, we would separate them with commas:

```
brain=User,Admin
```

You can assign your new user the User role by adding the appropriate line to the *roles.properties* file.

We will configure application security in Chapter 5.

What just happened?

You just added a user to the ToDo application using the default properties file-based authentication mechanism. Although JBoss doesn't provide a configuration-free way to add security to an application, we didn't have to change JBoss in any way to make use of the default mechanism.

Deploying the Application

Both the web and EJB sides of the application are ready. It is possible to deploy the WAR and EJB JAR files created directly to JBoss, but that would require a few more additional configuration steps to link the two parts of the application together. Instead, we'll assemble the application into an EAR file for deployment. It's not only better design, it's also easier.

How do I do that?

When you build the application, a *todo.ear* file is created in the *build/jars* directory. The EAR file combines the *todo.jar* and *todo.war* archives into one larger package. The structure is simple:

```
[todo]$ jar tf build/jars/todo.ear
META-INF/
META-INF/application.xml
todo.jar
todo.war
```

All that is required is a J2EE *application.xml* deployment descriptor. XDoclet doesn't generate it, but it is easy enough to produce by hand:

```
<application xmlns="http://java.sun.com/xml/ns/j2ee" version="1.4"
    xmlns:xsi="http://www.w3.org/2001/XMLSchema-instance"
    xsi:schemaLocation="http://java.sun.com/xml/ns/j2ee
                    http://java.sun.com/xml/ns/j2ee/application_1_4.xsd">
    <display-name>JBoss Notebook ToDo Application</display-name>
    <description>JBoss Notebook ToDo Application</description>
    <module>
        <ejb>todo.jar</ejb>
    </module>
    <module>
```

In the absence of explicit configuration, JBoss uses the base name of the WAR file as the context root.

```
        <web>
            <web-uri>todo.war</web-uri>
            <context-root>todo</context-root>
        </web>
    </module>
</application>
```

The deployment descriptor lists the archives, and in the case of the WAR file it adds the context root of the application telling JBoss what URL space the application serves. The context root is set to todo, which is what JBoss would have used had we deployed the *todo.war* file separately.

To deploy the application, copy the EAR file to the JBoss *deploy* directory. To get the Ant build file to do this for you, you should set the jboss.dir property to the location of your JBoss install directory:

```
<property name="jboss.dir" location="/tmp/jboss-4.0.2" />
```

Running the deploy target copies the EAR file out to the *deploy* directory of the default configuration:

```
[todo]$ ant deploy
Buildfile: build.xml

deploy:
    [copy] Copying 1 file to /tmp/jboss-4.0.2/server/default/deploy

BUILD SUCCESSFUL
Total time: 2 seconds
```

When you do this, you will see the results of your deployment in the console window:

Remember that deployment in JBoss is just a simple copy.

```
00:58:37,011 INFO  [EARDeployer] Init J2EE application: file:/private/tmp/
jboss-4.0.2/server/default/deploy/todo.ear
00:58:37,857 INFO  [EjbModule] Deploying Task
00:58:37,881 INFO  [EjbModule] Deploying Comment
00:58:37,917 INFO  [EjbModule] Deploying TaskMaster
00:58:38,482 INFO  [EJBDeployer] Deployed: file:/private/tmp/jboss-4.0.2/
server/default/tmp/deploy/tmp15658todo.ear-contents/todo.jar
00:58:38,543 INFO  [TomcatDeployer] deploy, ctxPath=/todo, warUrl=file:/
private/tmp/jboss-4.0.2/server/default/tmp/deploy/tmp15658todo.ear-contents/
todo.war/
00:58:39,664 WARN  [Digester] [NavigationRuleRule]{faces-config/navigation-
rule} Merge(*)
00:58:40,477 INFO  [EARDeployer] Started J2EE application: file:/private/
tmp/jboss-4.0.2/server/default/deploy/todo.ear
```

You can see JBoss generates a log message for each bean that is deployed. The Deploying Task, Deploying Comment, and Deploying TaskMaster messages confirm that those beans were successfully deployed. The Tomcat deployer logs a message telling us that the web application has been deployed and is indeed serving the /todo context root. Finally, the `Started J2EE application` message lets us know that the application as a whole has completed its deployment.

All that is left is to try and access the application. Since the application is serving the `/todo` context root, the full application can be accessed at *http://localhost:8080/todo/*.

When prompted to log in, enter a name and password from the *users. properties* file. Once you do that, the Figure 3-1 shows the application in action.

Figure 3-1. The ToDo application

J2EE with no configuration? It hardly seems possible.

The application supports task comments and a few other simple operations. But the most important thing is that the application is really up and running in JBoss.

What just happened?

The ToDo application has been deployed and all the J2EE services are functioning. Transactions and security are wired up and JBoss has even created the database tables in which it needs to store entity bean data. That last feature is pretty amazing, considering we haven't configured anything related to the database yet. In fact, it is interesting enough that we should spend a little more time looking at how JBoss is storing the EJB data.

Examining the Database

JBoss provides an embedded relational database called Hypersonic, and it automatically links CMP entity beans to that database in the absence of any other configuration. Using Hypersonic was a big help in getting an application up quickly. But instead of treating it like a big black box, we'll take a little time to dig into it a bit and understand exactly what JBoss is doing with the database.

How do I do that?

The console is at http://localhost:8080/jmx-console, if you forgot.

The Hypersonic database instance is completely embedded in JBoss and offers no connectivity to the world outside of the JBoss server, at least not by default. That means there is no convenient way to access the database from outside of JBoss. It does offer a simple management console, but we will need some co-operation from JBoss to get it running.

Fortunately for everyone, all services in JBoss are represented by managed beans (MBeans). The MBean for Hypersonic is responsible for interfacing with the database. You can get to the Hypersonic MBean using the JMX Console. You can load the JMX Console and then locate the `database=localDB,service=Hypersonic` MBean in the `jboss` domain.

Following the link provides the list of attributes and operations available. If you look around a bit, you will notice a `startDatabaseManager` operation. Invoking this operation launches the HSQL Database Manager, shown in Figure 3-2.

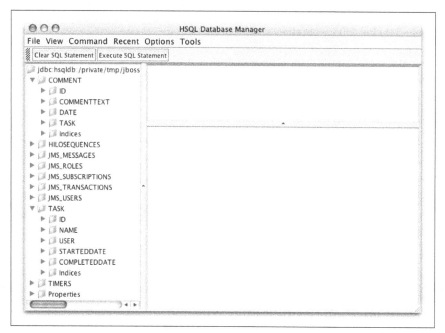

Figure 3-2. The HSQL Database Manager

The database manager is not an applet. It is a swing-based tool that is launched from within the JBoss instance. Even if you invoke the operation on a remote machine, the database manager runs on the machine that is actually running JBoss. This can be confusing if you are developing on a remote machine or if you are trying to run JBoss under a different user on the same machine, but it won't cause a problem for a typical development scenario.

On a Unix or Linux machine, you can set the DISPLAY environment variable when you start JBoss to control where the windows will be displayed.

The left pane of the application shows the tables available in the database. Of these, only the COMMENT and TASK tables are related to the ToDo application. The other tables are used for persistent JMS messages, timers, and sequence number generation. Hypersonic is the default datastore for everything in JBoss that needs to use a relational database.

JBoss has derived the table name for the entity beans from the bean's name. Drilling down on the table name lets you view the schema for the table. The CMP fields of the bean map to columns of the same name.

The task-to-comment relationship is a simple, one-to-many relationship that can be mapped using a foreign key. The TASK column on the COMMENT table provides this. If you examine the constraints under the Indices item, you'll see a primary key constraint on the ID field but no foreign key constraint on the TASK column. This is due to a shortcoming of CMP entity beans. JBoss does give you the ability to work around this limitation, but most J2EE developers have learned to simply work without foreign keys.

You can issue SQL statements by typing them into the text box in the right pane and clicking Execute SQL Statement. The results will be shown in a column view below the text box, as shown in Figure 3-3

You should be able to view and modify the data you have entered here. Try updating the name of a task and reloading the view in the web application. You might notice that the default caching policy for entity beans does not cache data in memory between requests.

What just happened?

We'll change databases in Chapter 4.

We've interacted with the Hypersonic database a bit more. Using the Hypersonic Database Manager, we've seen the default schema that JBoss created. We've also seen how to issue queries to inspect the data that's created. We didn't look at performance tuning or advanced configuration because Hypersonic is not the database you would want to use much further than the initial stages of development. It is, however, the perfect choice for the initial rapid development of J2EE applications.

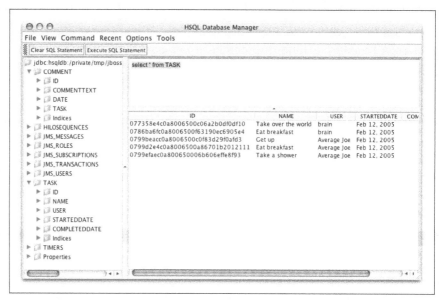

Figure 3-3. Viewing tables in Hypersonic

The data and tables created survive the redeployment, and even the undeployment, of the application. This is both convenient and inconvenient for early development. It is easy to remove the tables by issuing DROP statements from the database manager tool, but that is a very manual process.

If that is a bit too heavy-handed, JBoss provides a much more elegant solution to schema management. We'll look at that in Chapter 7.

A simpler, brute-force method is to just delete the Hypersonic *data* directory from the disk. The *data* directory in the server configuration contains permanent storage for many JBoss services. The Hypersonic database uses the *hypersonic* subdirectory to store its persistent data.

    [jboss-4.0.2]$ rm -rf server/default/data/hypersonic/

You should do this only with the JBoss server stopped. Hypersonic caches data in memory, and deleting the data while it is running may cause problems.

CHAPTER 4

Connecting to a Real Database

Modern enterprise applications revolve around relational databases, and our application is no exception. However, up to this point we have barely paid any attention to configuring the all-important database tier. We've been using the embedded Hypersonic database and delegating all the schema management to JBoss. This has allowed us to focus on making our application work first, without needing to bother with the added complexity of a database.

Developing an application with this approach makes a lot of sense, but now that our application is up and running, it's time to turn our attention toward the database, and have our application access a more robust, production-friendly database. We'll use MySQL for the application.

Setting Up MySQL

MySQL is a free download that is available from *http://dev.mysql.com* for every major computing platform. You'll want to download and install the most current MySQL distribution available for your platform. We'll be working from the MySQL Standard 4.1.8 GA version.

We'll assume you can follow the instructions for installing MySQL on your platform. Once you have MySQL running, you'll need to create a database to be used by JBoss. You'll also need to create a database user that has access to the JBoss database for JBoss to use.

How do I do that?

MySQL is administered using the `mysql` command found in your MySQL installation. On our machine it is found in */usr/local/mysql/bin/mysql*.

You'll want to run with the `mysql` client as the root user, using the `-u` option:

```
$ /usr/local/mysql/bin/mysql -u root
Welcome to the MySQL monitor.  Commands end with ; or \g.
Your MySQL connection id is 4 to server version: 4.1.8-standard

Type 'help;' or '\h' for help. Type '\c' to clear the buffer.

mysql>
```

After connecting to the database, we'll create a database named `jbossdb`, using the `create database` command:

```
mysql> create database jbossdb;
Query OK, 1 row affected (0.01 sec)
```

Now we need to create a user account to be used when accessing the `jbossdb` database. The `grant` command accomplishes this:

```
mysql> grant all privileges on jbossdb.* to todoapp@localhost identified
by 'secretpassword';
Query OK, 0 rows affected (0.38 sec)
```

This creates a user called `todoapp` whose password is `secretpassword`. This user is granted full rights to everything in the `jbossdb` database when connecting from the same host. You can examine the `mysql.user` table to verify that the user was created correctly:

```
mysql> select user,host,password from mysql.user;
+-----------+------------+-------------------------------------------+
| user      | host       | password                                  |
+-----------+------------+-------------------------------------------+
| root      | localhost  |                                           |
| root      | toki.local |                                           |
|           | toki.local |                                           |
|           | localhost  |                                           |
| todoapp   | localhost  | *F89FFE84BFC48A876BC682C4C23ABA4BF64711A4 |
+-----------+------------+-------------------------------------------+
6 rows in set (0.00 sec)
```

If you want to run MySQL on a different host, you need to give the database user access from the host JBoss is running on.

Note that `todoapp` only has permission to access the database locally, and has no remote access. You can test the username and password using the `-u` and `-password` options:

```
$ /usr/local/mysql/bin/mysql -u todoapp --password=secretpassword
```

You can also test remote access to the database by running the `mysql` command from a remote machine, using the `-h` option to specify the machine that is running MySQL. Since we've only granted access from `localhost`, the access attempts should fail.

What just happened?

You've created a database to be used by JBoss, and you've created a user who has permission to access the database. You don't need to worry about creating special tables or loading any data. JBoss will take care of creating the database tables needed.

Adding the JDBC Driver

As mature as relational database technologies are, there is still no standard network protocol for accessing them. JDBC saves us from needing to couple our application to proprietary database APIs by letting us hide the proprietary access protocols behind a nice, standard Java interface. To do that, we will need to provide the JDBC driver code to JBoss.

How do I do that?

The first step is to locate the JDBC driver code. The MySQL driver is called MySql Connector/J. The current production version is Connector/J 3.0, which you can download from *http://www.mysql.com/products/connector/j/*. The driver JAR file is located inside of the archive you downloaded. For the 3.0.16 version, which is current as of this writing, the name of the file is *mysql-connector-java-3.0.16-ga-bin.jar*.

Once you've located the JDBC JAR file, you will need to copy it to the *lib* directory of your JBoss server configuration. As you recall, we are working from the default configuration, so that would be *server/default/lib*.

The decision to make a library JAR file static or hot deployable is always tough.

What just happened?

Well, nothing happened. We've talked about the hot deploy feature of JBoss, but that works only for items placed in the *deploy* directory. The *lib* directory works differently. JARs in the *lib* directory are added to the topmost JBoss classloader and cannot be redeployed or removed. The *lib* directory is ignored after JBoss starts up. The only way to get JBoss to notice the new JDBC driver is to restart the server, so you'll need to shut down and restart your JBoss instance after installing the driver.

How do we know that JBoss has found our driver? We would hope that JBoss would give us some kind of warning or error when we try to use the database connection, but that is a very delayed form of feedback when we haven't yet seen how to use the new database.

There is a solution, though. We'll use the JMX Console to check on our class. Open the JMX Console in your web browser (*http://localhost:8080/ jmx-console*). Near the top of the screen you will see the JMImplementation domain, which has three managed beans (MBeans), as shown here:

```
JMImplementation
    • name=Default,service=LoaderRepository
    • type=MBeanRegistry
    • type=MBeanServerDelegate
```

Selecting the Loader repository brings you to the management interface for the loader repository (see Figure 4-1).

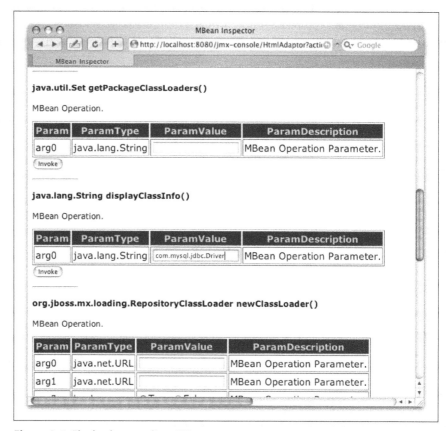

Figure 4-1. The loader repository MBean

We can use the displayClassInfo operation, which is shown in Figure 4-1, to find out what JBoss knows about the class. The operation takes a Java class name as input, so enter the name of our MySQL driver (com.mysql.jdbc.Driver) and click the Invoke button. The MBean will respond with the following text:

You can use this to check whether any class is visible in JBoss.

```
com.mysql.jdbc.Driver Information
Not loaded in repository cache
```

```
### Instance0 found in UCL: org.jboss.mx.loading.UnifiedClassLoader3@f8d6a6
...
```

We haven't used the class yet, so JBoss has not yet loaded the class into memory. However, it can see that the driver class is visible in one of JBoss's classloaders. If JBoss had already loaded the class, we would have gotten much more information back from the displayClassInfo operation, as shown in the following listing:

```
com.mysql.jdbc.Driver Information
Repository cache version:
com.mysql.jdbc.Driver(85d49e).ClassLoader=org.jboss.mx.loading.
UnifiedClassLoader3@
f8d6a6{ url=file:/private/tmp/jboss-4.0.2/server/default/tmp/deploy/tmp14828jboss-
service.xml ,addedOrder=2}
..org.jboss.mx.loading.UnifiedClassLoader3@f8d6a6{ url=file:/private/tmp/jboss-
4.0.2/server/default/tmp/deploy/tmp14828jboss-service.xml ,addedOrder=2}
....file:/private/tmp/jboss-4.0.2/server/default/tmp/deploy/tmp14828jboss-service.xml
....file:/private/tmp/jboss-4.0.2/server/default/lib/activation.jar
....file:/private/tmp/jboss-4.0.2/server/default/lib/avalon-framework.jar
....file:/private/tmp/jboss-4.0.2/server/default/lib/bcel.jar
...
++++CodeSource:
  (file:/private/tmp/jboss-4.0.2/server/default/lib/mysql-connector-
  java-3.0.16-ga-bin.jar )
Implemented Interfaces:
```

```
### Instance0 found in UCL: org.jboss.mx.loading.UnifiedClassLoader3@f8d6a6
```

Class loading can be tricky, but JBoss provides all the tools you need to understand what is going on.

This tells us that we have indeed loaded the MySQL driver into memory, and JBoss is using the version from the JAR file we put in *server/default/lib*. This might seem like a lot more detail than we want, but when you have different versions of JARs in different packages and are trying to understand exactly how your classes are being loaded, the extra information is invaluable. But for now, we just want to know that JBoss can locate our driver class.

What about...

...placing the JDBC driver in the *deploy* directory?

It certainly seems harsh that we had to restart JBoss to make it see our little JDBC driver. Why can't we just put the JDBC driver in the *deploy* directory and let it be hot deployed? Well, we could have. And it would work almost the same. However, it's generally accepted that it's better to put fundamental service code in the *lib* directory. JAR files in the *deploy* directory will be redeployed if you accidentally touch them, through an automated build script, for example. That can create havoc if several applications share the JDBC driver.

We really just don't think of a JDBC driver as being an application component. It's generally thought of as system-level code and is placed with the other system-level JAR files in the *lib* directory. However, if it's more convenient, feel free to put the JDBC driver along with your application code in the *deploy* directory.

Creating a Datasource

With a database running and the drivers loaded, the application could connect directly to the database and issue queries if we wanted it to. But in a J2EE world we don't need to do that. JBoss, like all J2EE application servers, can manage database connections for us, allowing us to write our applications free of the need to configure connections or maintain connection pools ourselves.

Even though we haven't specified the datasource for the ToDo application, JBoss has connected us to a default datasource called, conveniently enough, DefaultDS. It connects to our embedded Hypersonic database. Now we want to create a new datasource definition that will connect to the MySQL database we created in the first lab.

How do I do that?

In JBoss, a datasource is a deployable entity just like our application WAR and EAR files. It is represented by a special **-ds.xml* file in the *deploy* directory. The Hypersonic datasource is configured in the *hsqldb-ds.xml* file. We'll look at that as an example. Here's an abbreviated version of it:

```xml
<?xml version="1.0" encoding="UTF-8"?>

<datasources>
   <local-tx-datasource>
      <jndi-name>DefaultDS</jndi-name>

      <connection-url>
         jdbc:hsqldb:${jboss.server.data.dir}${/}hypersonic${/}localDB
      </connection-url>
      <driver-class>org.hsqldb.jdbcDriver</driver-class>
```

```
            <user-name>sa</user-name>
            <password></password>

            <min-pool-size>5</min-pool-size>
            <max-pool-size>20</max-pool-size>
            <idle-timeout-minutes>0</idle-timeout-minutes>
            <track-statements/>

            <security-domain>HsqlDbRealm</security-domain>

            <metadata>
                <type-mapping>Hypersonic SQL</type-mapping>
            </metadata>

            <depends>jboss:service=Hypersonic,database=localDB</depends>
        </local-tx-datasource>
    </datasources>
```

External clients can't look up a datasource and use it.

While there is a bit of noise in the file, it's pretty easy to guess what is going on. This datasource is named DefaultDS. It's bound under the JNDI name java:DefaultDS, meaning that it, like everything in the java: context, is only available inside the JVM. You can also see the connection URL and the database username and password, as well as a few other minor connection pool details.

It's really a simple format, and it would be pretty easy to duplicate this file, adding the connection details for our MySQL database. But it's even easier than that. The *docs/examples/jca* directory (under the root of your JBoss installation, not the server configuration directory you are working in) contains sample templates for the most popular database servers (and most of the less popular ones too).

The MySQL template is *mysql-ds.xml*:

```
<?xml version="1.0" encoding="UTF-8"?>

<!-- $Id$ -->
<!-- Datasource config for MySQL using 3.0.9 available from:
http://www.mysql.com/downloads/api-jdbc-stable.html
-->

<datasources>
  <local-tx-datasource>
    <jndi-name>MySqlDS</jndi-name>
    <connection-url>jdbc:mysql://mysql-hostname:3306/jbossdb</connection-url>
    <driver-class>com.mysql.jdbc.Driver</driver-class>
    <user-name>x</user-name>
    <password>y</password>

    <!-- corresponding type-mapping in the
         standardjbosscmp-jdbc.xml (optional) -->
```

```
            <metadata>
                <type-mapping>mySQL</type-mapping>
            </metadata>
        </local-tx-datasource>

    </datasources>
```

To get started, you need to copy *mysql-ds.xml* to the *deploy* directory and change the items in bold to the correct values for the server. The MySQL JNDI name is fine, so we'll start with `connection-url`. We'll assume that our database is located on the same machine as our JBoss instance, so we'll use `localhost` as the machine name.

```
<connection-url>jdbc:mysql://localhost:3306/jbossdb</connection-url>
```

The only other step is to tell JBoss the database user to connect as. We used the user `todoapp`, so we'll specify that, and the password, here:

```
<user-name>todoapp</user-name>
<password>secretpassword</password>
```

What just happened?

You've now deployed a datasource in JBoss. You can look to the console log to make sure everything went right. If all went well, you'll see a line that looks like the following:

<aside>You should profile your application to determine the optimal connection pool size.</aside>

```
20:09:23,756 INFO [WrapperDataSourceService] Bound connection factory for resource
adapter for ConnectionManager 'jboss.jca
name=MySqlDS,service=DataSourceBinding to
JNDI name 'java:MySqlDS'
```

If you've edited and saved the file a few times, the console should show that you've redeployed it several times. We'll make one more change, explicitly specifying the datasource connection pool size, and watch it redeploy.

Since we don't expect much traffic, we'll ask JBoss to keep just two connections ready in the pool, and to keep a maximum of ten connections open. To do that, add the following `min-pool-size` and `max-pool-size` elements to your *mysql-ds.xml* file:

```
<?xml version="1.0" encoding="UTF-8"?>

<!-- $Id$ -->
<!-- Datasource config for MySQL using 3.0.9 available from:
http://www.mysql.com/downloads/api-jdbc-stable.html
-->
<datasources>
    <local-tx-datasource>
        <jndi-name>MySqlDS</jndi-name>
```

```
<connection-url>jdbc:mysql://mysql-hostname:3306/jbossdb
</connection-url>
<driver-class>com.mysql.jdbc.Driver</driver-class>
<user-name>todoapp</user-name>
<password>secretpassword</password>

<min-pool-size>2</min-pool-size>
<max-pool-size>10</max-pool-size>

<!-- corresponding type-mapping in the
     standardjbosscmp-jdbc.xml (optional) -->
<metadata>
    <type-mapping>mySQL</type-mapping>
</metadata>
</local-tx-datasource>

</datasources>
```

When you save the file you'll see that the datasource successfully redeployed in the console log. This is all the feedback JBoss gives you
directly. In the "Monitoring the Connection Pool" lab later in this chapter,
we'll see how to verify our pool size and check on other aspects of the
connection pool, such as how many connections are in use. For a full set
of configuration options, see *jboss-ds_1_5.dtd* in the *docs/dtd* directory.
Other template datasource descriptors are located in *docs/examples/jca*.

What about...

...making our datasource be `DefaultDS`?

That is possible. If we removed `hsql-ds.xml` and changed our datasource JNDI name to `DefaultDS`, JBoss would use our MySQL database as
the default for all applications. However, keep in mind that internal services such as JMS use `DefaultDS`. While they can be easily configured to
use other databases, and indeed they should be if we are deploying a
production server using those services, it's generally better to be explicit
about which datasource you are using.

And what about XA datasources?

You might be wondering what the `local-tx-datasource` element means
in the datasource file. It means that the datasource only supports local
transactions and can't be combined with other resources in a true dis-
tributed (XA) transaction. If your database supports XA (MySQL doesn't),
you can change the `local-tx-datasource` tag to `xa-datasource`. Examples of XA datasource configurations are available in *docs/examples/jca*
and are named `*-xa-ds.xml`.

*XA datasources
are a real pain.
Just because your
database and
driver claim to
support XA
transactions
doesn't mean it
really works. If
you plan to use XA
transactions,
make sure to test
them thoroughly.*

Linking the Datasource to Our Application

With the datasource in place, we need to tell our application to use it. The amount of effort involved depends on how coupled our application is to the datasource. If an application used the datasource directly, we would need to adjust the lookup code, or at least the environment references, and update our SQL statements to be compatible with MySQL. Fortunately for us, the ToDo application uses container-managed persistence and the database access is completely transparent. So, migrating the application will be quite simple.

How do I do that?

This one is going to be easy. JBoss looks for the container-managed persistence configuration in a jbosscmp-jdbc.xml deployment descriptor. The default datasource for the application is set in the defaults section of the file, as shown here:

```
<!DOCTYPE jbosscmp-jdbc PUBLIC
    "-//JBoss//DTD JBOSSCMP-JDBC 4.0//EN"
    "http://www.jboss.org/j2ee/dtd/jbosscmp-jdbc_4_0.dtd">

<jbosscmp-jdbc>
    <defaults>
        <datasource>java:MySqlDS</datasource>
        <datasource-mapping>mySQL</datasource-mapping>
    </defaults>
</jbosscmp-jdbc>
```

The datasource element contains the JNDI name of the datasource we specified in the *mysql-ds.xml* file earlier. The datasource-mapping name declares the type of the database. The database type determines how to generate SQL and how to map types for a particular database.

You can look at the *conf/standardjbosscmp-jdbc.xml* file to see the full set of datasource mappings available in JBoss. Inside the type-mappings section, you should find the mySQL type mapping referenced in the *jbosscmp-jdbc.xml* file:

```
<type-mapping>
    <name>mySQL</name>
    ...
</type-mapping>
```

The type mapping defines SQL templates for schema generation, EJB-QL, and JBOSS-QL function mappings, as well as the default mapping for standard Java types. Here is the mapping for java.lang.String:

```
<mapping>
    <java-type>java.lang.String</java-type>
    <jdbc-type>VARCHAR</jdbc-type>
    <sql-type>VARCHAR(250) BINARY</sql-type>
</mapping>
```

If you need to change the mapping for strings for all MySQL databases in the system, you can edit the *standardjbosscmp-jdbc.xml* file. In general you'll probably want to edit the mapping on a field-by-field basis, but it is nice to know that you have the power to edit the systemwide mapping if need be.

The *jbosscmp-jdbc.xml* file is placed in the *META-INF* directory of the EJB JAR, right next to the ejb-jar.xml and jboss.xml deployment descriptors. In order to include the MySQL-specific *jbosscmp-jdbc.xml* file, add -Doptional.dd=mysql to the ant commands used to build the ToDo application, as shown here:

```
$ ant -Doptional.dd=mysql main deploy
```

This builds and deploys the MySQL version of the application.

What just happened?

The ToDo application is no longer speaking to the internal Hypersonic database. Instead it is speaking to the MySQL instance you set up. And just as before, JBoss automatically created the database schema appropriate for our entity beans. You can check to see that our tables were created correctly using the show tables command:

```
mysql> use jbossdb;
Database changed
mysql> show tables;
+--------------------+
| Tables_in_jbossdb |
+--------------------+
| Comment           |
| Task              |
+--------------------+
2 rows in set (0.19 sec)
```

You can check the generated schema for the table using the describe command:

```
mysql> describe task;
+----------------+----------------+------+-----+---------+-------+
| Field          | Type           | Null | Key | Default | Extra |
+----------------+----------------+------+-----+---------+-------+
| id             | varchar(250)   |      | PRI |         |       |
| name           | varchar(250)   | YES  |     | NULL    |       |
| user           | varchar(250)   | YES  |     | NULL    |       |
| startedDate    | datetime       | YES  |     | NULL    |       |
| completedDate  | datetime       | YES  |     | NULL    |       |
+----------------+----------------+------+-----+---------+-------+
5 rows in set (0.42 sec)
```

If you access the application and create a few tasks, you can easily query the data from the `mysql` tool and verify that everything is working:

```
mysql> select name,user,startedDate from task;
+--------------------+-------+---------------------+
| name               | user  | startedDate         |
+--------------------+-------+---------------------+
| take over the world | brain | 2005-01-18 00:50:29 |
| eat the box        | pinky | 2005-01-18 00:51:22 |
+--------------------+-------+---------------------+
2 rows in set (0.20 sec)
```

Monitoring the Connection Pool

We've spent all our time looking at how to create the datasource, but we haven't mentioned how you can interact with the underlying connection pool during the life of your application. You need to set up the datasource only once, but your application will use it every day. In this lab we will find the connection pool and see how to interact with its management interface to monitor and tune it.

How do I do that?

Each datasource declared in a *ds.xml* file translates into several MBeans that you can interact with in the JMX Console. All the datasource-related objects are in the `jboss.jca` domain. You can find them by searching through the JMX Console page, or by using `jboss.jca:*` as the query filter.

This is enough of a filter to spot the items related to the MySQL datasource, but you could use a more specific filter, such as `jboss.jca:name=MySqlDS,*`, to see only the MySQL entries. In either case, four MBeans will be related to the MySQL datasource:

- name=MySqlDS,service=DataSourceBinding
- name=MySqlDS,service=LocalTxCM
- name=MySqlDS,service=ManagedConnectionFactory
- name=MySqlDS,service=ManagedConnectionPool

While each plays a critical role in providing the datasource functionality in JBoss, you are most likely to need to interact with the connection pool. Click the connection pool MBean to expose the management attributes and operations.

The *mysql-ds.xml* file we've been using specified a minimum connection pool size of 2 and a maximum pool size of 10. You'll see those values reflected in the MinSize and MaxSize attributes. You can change the values in the running server by adjusting the values and clicking Apply Changes.

Setting the values here affects the connection pool only in memory. To change the configuration permanently, update the *mysql-ds.xml* file. Try setting the pool sizes there. When you save the file, JBoss will redeploy the datasource and the new pool sizes will be displayed when you reload the page.

You might occasionally want to adjust the pool size to account for usage; you are more likely to be curious how much of the connection pool is being used. The ConnectionCount attribute shows how many connections are currently open to the database. However, open connections are not necessarily in use by application code. The InUseConnectionCount attribute shows how many of the open connections are in use. Viewing the statistic from the other direction, AvailableConnectionCount shows how much room is left in the pool.

Finally, the MBean has several statistics that track connection pool usage over the pool's lifetime. ConnectionCreatedCount and Connection-DestroyedCount keep running totals of the number of connections created and destroyed by the pool. If IdleTimeout is greater than 0, connections will eventually timeout, be destroyed, and be replaced by fresh connections. This will cause the created and destroyed counts to rise constantly. The MaxConnectionsInUseCount attribute keeps track of the highest number of connections in use at a time.

If you notice anything awkward in the connection pool, or you just want to reset the statistics, you can flush the connection pool using the flush operation on the MBean. This will cause a new connection pool to be created, abandoning the previous connection pool.

We will use some of the more advanced monitoring and alerting features of the web console in Chapter 8.

What just happened?

You've seen a whole set of attributes that will prove invaluable when you need to understand how an application is using its database connections. All the MBean attributes are visible through the JMX management tool of your choice. We've used the JBoss JMX Console in this lab, but other options exist.

To give you a taste of what you can do, Figure 4-2 shows a graph of the ConnectionCount attribute over a short, 10-minute time period that we used the ToDo application. The graph was created by the JBoss Web Console application, the GUI companion to the JMX Console we've been using.

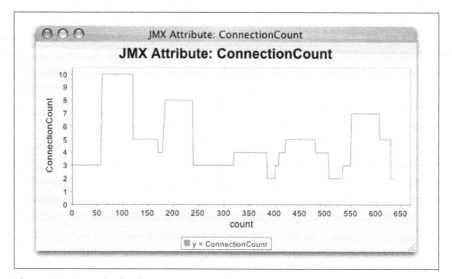

Figure 4-2. A graph of a datasource connection count

CHAPTER 5

Applying Security

In the ToDo application, we made several concessions both to fit into the J2EE notion of security and to live within the bounds of the default authentication mechanism provided by JBoss. That mechanism, if you recall, allows for the authentication of users using Java properties files. It's simple and quick. But although it's the perfect solution to get an application up and running quickly, we're willing to bet you won't want to deploy a real application with a user management process that involves manually editing files and redeploying your application.

In this chapter, we'll see how we can configure the behavior of JBoss to allow for much more interesting security policies around applications. We'll see how to make JBoss pull user and role information from a relational database and from an LDAP server, and we'll see how to combine login mechanisms to better fit the needs of a real application deployment. We'll also take a step back to the web tier and look at how to enable SSL support for secure access to applications.

Defining a Security Domain

The action of authenticating the user (verifying the user's password) and authorizing the user (checking whether the user has permissions to perform a given action) comes from something called a security domain. The ToDo application supplies user information in the *users.properties* and *roles.properties* files, but this works only because JBoss provides a default security domain that knows to look for those files. In this section, we'll override the default security domain and provide an explicit security configuration that can be customized later to meet the application's security needs.

How do I do that?

The *conf/login-config.xml* file is the central configuration point for security in JBoss. It provides the policies that define each security domain. Take a look through the file. You will see a collection of application-policy elements that declare the security domains in JBoss. Here is an example found near the end of the file:

```
<!--
    The default login configuration used by any security domain that
    does not have an application-policy entry with a matching name
-->
<application-policy name="other">
    <authentication>
        <login-module
            code="org.jboss.security.auth.spi.UsersRolesLoginModule"
            flag="required" />
    </authentication>
</application-policy>
```

This defines a security domain named other. It defines an authentication system that uses UsersRolesLoginModule, which reads user and role information from the simple properties files we have been using. The other security domain is the default security domain for the system. When JBoss doesn't find a security domain configured for the application, it uses this one.

If you want to change the authentication policy, you can make the change to the other security domain. However, this will change the default policy for the entire server, which likely is not the best strategy. A better strategy is to declare a new security domain. To do that, you need to create a new policy based on the original policy. Add the following policy to the *login-config.xml* file:

```
<application-policy name="todo">
    <authentication>
        <login-module
            code="org.jboss.security.auth.spi.UsersRolesLoginModule"
            flag="required" />
    </authentication>
</application-policy>
```

This declares a new security domain named todo. You'll need to restart the server for JBoss to see the changes to the file and recognize the new domain.

What happens when a security domain falls in the forest but no applications are around to hear it? That's the state the application is in. JBoss doesn't know that the ToDo application needs the todo security domain.

Unless you specify otherwise, JBoss will continue to use the other domain.

To set the security domain, we need to introduce another JBoss-specific deployment descriptor, *jboss-web.xml*. *jboss-web.xml* sits next to the standard *web.xml* file in the *WEB*-INF directory of the WAR file and provides additional deployment information.

To link to a specific security domain, you need to set the security-domain element to the JNDI name of the security domain to link to. Security domains are bound under `java:/jaas` in JNDI, so the todo domain would be `java:/jaas/todo`, as shown here:

```
<!DOCTYPE jboss-web PUBLIC
        "-//JBoss//DTD Web Application 2.4//EN"
        "http://www.jboss.org/j2ee/dtd/jboss-web_4_0.dtd">
<jboss-web>
    <security-domain>java:/jaas/todo</security-domain>
</jboss-web>
```

Using the -Doptional.dd=security flag when you invoke the build script includes the descriptor in the *jboss-web.xml* file in *todo.war*:

```
[todo]$ ant -Doptional.dd=security
```

What just happened?

You created a new security domain named todo, backed by UsersRolesLoginModule, which replicates the functionality of the default security domain. Although this module is simple to set up, it is not very flexible to deploy. However, now that you have explicitly created the security domain and linked it to the application, you can swap out the login modules with any other implementation you desire, a process that is completely transparent to the application.

Using a Relational Database for Users

Nearly every J2EE application stores data in a relational database, so it is natural to want to store user data in the database alongside your existing data. It's likely that your domain models contain a user object that already captures the concept of a login name and password, if not full role data. We've chosen not to have a user object in the ToDo application to ensure maximum flexibility, but chances are you'll want to control user information dynamically using data in the database.

You can use the same security domain element in other JBoss deployment descriptors, such as jboss.xml.

If the J2EE specification defined a user management API, we wouldn't have to make these kinds of trade-offs.

How do I do that?

First you need to get user and role data into the database. Since we don't have a user domain object to work from, we'll need to create new tables in the database. We'll create one table for storing the user information, and a separate table for storing the role data. Open the Hypersonic database manager tool and create the following two tables:

```
CREATE TABLE USERS(login VARCHAR(64) PRIMARY KEY, passwd VARCHAR(64))
CREATE TABLE USER_ROLES(login VARCHAR(64), role VARCHAR(32))
```

You can store user information in the database in many ways. You might have user ID and role ID columns, for example, for a more normalized database structure. As we'll see later, JBoss doesn't really care how you structure the data. As long as you can create efficient SQL queries to extract user and role information, you'll be able to work with the data easily within JBoss.

While you have the database manager open, you should also add the users to the database:

```
INSERT into USERS values('pinky', 'duh')
INSERT into USERS values('brain', 'conquest')
INSERT into USER_ROLES values('pinky', 'User')
INSERT into USER_ROLES values('brain', 'User')
```

Now we will update the security domain in the *login-config.xml* file. DatabaseServerLoginModule provides the ability to load user and role data from a database. So, we'll use it:

```
<application-policy name="todo">
    <authentication>
        <login-module
              code="org.jboss.security.auth.spi.DatabaseServerLoginModule"
              flag="required">
            <module-option name="dsJndiName">java:/DefaultDS</module-option>
            <module-option name="principalsQuery">
                select passwd from USERS where login=?
            </module-option>
            <module-option name="rolesQuery">
                select role, 'Roles' from USER_ROLES where login=?
            </module-option>
        </login-module>
    </authentication>
</application-policy>
```

Don't forget to restart the server when you modify login-config.xml.

This login module needs three configuration parameters. The dsJndiName attribute is the JNDI name of the datasource to use. If you use a different database, it's a simple matter to change the name to bind the login module to your database of choice.

The `principalsQuery` and `rolesQuery` attributes provide the SQL queries to extract the user and role information from the database. You can use any SQL that makes sense for your database and user data, as long as the queries return result data in the form that the login module expects.

Basically, you provide the schema and the queries.

The `principalsQuery` attribute should return a single row with a single column that contains the password for the user. The `rolesQuery` attribute is slightly more complicated. It should return rows that contain two columns. The first column should be the role name, and the second should be the name of the JAAS principal to use. To provide role data, this should simply be `Roles`. It's rare to need to delve into the depths of JAAS, so it's enough to hardcode the `Roles` value in the query and not worry about it.

What just happened?

You moved the user login information from the hardcoded properties files to the database using `DatabaseServerLoginModule`. All you needed to do was to add the user information to the database and configure the database login module to read it.

Moving user information into the database makes the data easy to inspect and manage. When user information in the database changes, that information can be used immediately at the application level. After adding a user to the database, for example, that user should be able to log in immediately.

Changes, on the other hand, are a bit trickier. The security manager caches authentication credentials so that it doesn't have to consult the database on every single access to the web page. This is great for performance, but it can sometimes leave you scratching your head, wondering why JBoss isn't recognizing changed passwords or new group information. If you need to force JBoss to see changes to data, invoke the `flushAuthenticationCache` operation on the `JAASSecurityManager` MBean after updating the data.

Using Hashed Passwords

Storing plain-text passwords, whether in local files or in the database, can be worrisome. Even if you take care to protect the resources, exposing passwords in plain text is always a concern. The login modules we have seen so far allow for password hashes to be used in place of plain-text passwords.

You can think of a hashed password as an encrypted form of a password that can't be decrypted. If someone were to obtain the hashed password, they would have no way to recover the original password. To verify that a user's password is correct, you can apply the hash function to the value and see if the resulting hashed value is the same as the stored hash value. If it is, the password is correct. Using hashed passwords doesn't guarantee the security of your passwords, but it does help keep them out of plain sight.

How do I do that?

To use hashed passwords, you must configure the login module to use the desired hashing algorithm. Additionally, since hashed passwords are binary data, you will need to decide how the passwords will be encoded as text strings. Both of those configuration options are set as options on the login module.

Here is the login module from the previous lab, with password hashing enabled:

```
<application-policy name="todo">
    <authentication>
        <login-module
            code="org.jboss.security.auth.spi.DatabaseServerLoginModule"
            flag="required">
            <module-option name="dsJndiName">
                java:/DefaultDS</module-option>
            <module-option name="principalsQuery">
                select passwd from USERS where login=?
            </module-option>
            <module-option name="rolesQuery">
                select role, 'Roles' from USER_ROLES where login=?
            </module-option>
            <module-option name="hashAlgorithm">MD5</module-option>
            <module-option name="hashEncoding">BASE64</module-option>
        </login-module>
    </authentication>
</application-policy>
```

Base64 encoding produces text strings that are more compact than hex- (Base16) encoded ones.

hashAlgorithm tells us the name of the message digest algorithm to use. We've used MD5 here. Another commonly used message digest algorithm is SHA. You can use any message digest algorithm supported by your JCE provider. The hashEncoding value is used to translate the binary hash into a string value. JBoss supports Base64 and hex encoding.

With this configuration, the login module expects to find hashed passwords in the database instead of plain-text passwords. But how do you get the hashed passwords there? Your user management code will need to take care of that. Since the algorithm and encoding methods are standard, this isn't hard to do. The following code uses the org.jboss.security.Util helper class to create a hashed password using MD5 and Base64 encoding:

```
import org.jboss.security.Util;

public class Hash
{
    public static void main(String[ ] args)
        throws Exception
    {
        if (args.length != 1) {
            System.out.println("ARGS: password");
            return;
        }

        String password = args[0];
        String result   = Util.createPasswordHash("MD5",
                                        Util.BASE64_ENCODING,
                                        null,
                                        null,
                                        password);

        System.out.println("MD5(" + password +")=" + result);

    }
}
```

If you need to generate just a few passwords for test purposes, OpenSSL is a good cross-platform tool. It supports both MD5 and SHA digests as well as Base64 encoding. Here are examples that illustrate both of these digest algorithms:

```
[hash]$ echo -n mypassword | openssl dgst -md5 -binary | openssl base64
NIGde+6ruSYKXIVLyFs+RA==
[hash]$ echo -n mypassword | openssl dgst -sha -binary | openssl base64
eJrcMNO1ZfbtLMPmcsR7bOJRvk4=
```

See http://www.openssl.org/ for more information about OpenSSL.

You can put these values directly into the passwd column of a user in the database. Once you update the plain-text values in the database with the hashed values, you will be able to access the ToDo application again.

What just happened?

You switched from using plain-text passwords to using hashed passwords. You can use password hashing with almost all of the JBoss-provided login modules. In each case the configuration options are exactly the same.

Don't be careless with hashed passwords. You should still treat them as confidential information.

We'll repeat a point we made earlier. Hashed passwords don't guarantee security. Weak passwords are still susceptible to dictionary attacks, for example. Furthermore, the hashing mechanism supported by JBoss doesn't use any form of salt, which means that two users with the same password will have the same hashed value. None of this is to say that hashed passwords are not valuable. They are. However, don't assume that just because you are using them you don't need to take care of your password data.

Our Approach to Application Security

J2EE security is so limited as to be almost entirely useless. You can count on it to restrict access to your application, but it doesn't help much with the fine-grained user-based or object-based access control policies you generally want to apply in an application. In other words, J2EE security helps you say "only valid users should be able to use the application," but it doesn't help you say "users should only be able edit objects they created."

JBoss provides some limited help in implementing instance-based security by allowing you to define a SecurityProxy for each bean type. You can implement any sort of access policy you want in the proxy, and JBoss will make sure that your policy is consulted before each access to a bean.

The SecurityProxy does keep your application code free of instance-based security checks, but you still manage the security details yourself at the presentation tier. Thinking about the ToDo application, a SecurityProxy could enforce the rule that users can only modify their own tasks, but it would be rather rude of the application to present a user with the option to edit a task only to fail when he tries to save it because that security policy is only reflected in the bean.

There's nothing in J2EE, or in JBoss, that provides a real framework for full application security. You are on your own to implement the policy that makes the most sense. In the ToDo application, we've decided not to worry about bean-level security. The beans are entirely local to the application, so we've chosen to just apply security at the presentation tier.

When displaying the task list, the controller only asks for tasks for a specific user. Only those tasks are displayed to the user, and the user can only edit those tasks. Assuming the presentation tier cannot be hacked to allow access to objects other than the ones presented to the user, this is sufficient to limit access to the application. If you don't want to rely on the presentation tier as the only implementation of the security policy, you could couple it with a SecurityProxy on the EJBs to provide the hard enforcement of rules.

Using an LDAP Server for Users

Storing user information in a relational database along with your other application data is a great strategy when your application controls the user data. However, user data often needs to be shared between applications or managed by external systems. In these cases, an LDAP directory server is frequently called upon to be the central repository for user information. If you are faced with a central LDAP user repository, you'll be relieved to know that the LDAP login module is just as easy to use as the ones we've seen so far.

LDAP makes sense only if you need to share information between systems. Don't introduce LDAP just to manage information for one application.

How do I do that?

LDAP has some truly wonderful features. It has a standard network protocol and a standard query mechanism, which guarantees that any client can talk to any server without the need for vendor-proprietary drivers or customized queries. LDAP also has standardized schemas, which allow for standard data representations between servers.

It might seem like LDAP is the Holy Grail of standardized user management. Unfortunately, it doesn't quite work out that way. With all of the flexibility LDAP offers, nearly every LDAP system has its own twist on representing users. As a result, LDAP login modules always require a significant amount of configuration to make them work. And, despite the differences, there's enough in common that a simple example aptly illustrates how to map your user data into information that JBoss can use to authenticate and authorize users.

Here is an LDAP data interchange format (LDIF) file that contains the data we'll be working from in this lab:

```
dn: o=jbossnotebook
objectclass: top
objectclass: organization
o: jbossnotebook

dn: ou=People,o=jbossnotebook
objectclass: top
objectclass: organizationalUnit
ou: People

dn: uid=norman,ou=People,o=jbossnotebook
objectclass: top
objectclass: uidObject
objectclass: person
uid: norman
```

```
cn: Norman
sn: Richards
userPassword: secretpassword1

dn: uid=sam,ou=People,o=jbossnotebook
objectclass: top
objectclass: uidObject
objectclass: person
uid: sam
cn: Sam
sn: Griffith
userPassword: secretpassword2

dn: ou=Roles,o=jbossnotebook
objectclass: top
objectclass: organizationalUnit
ou: Roles

dn: cn=User,ou=Roles,o=jbossnotebook
objectclass: top
objectclass: groupOfNames
cn: User
member: uid=norman,ou=People,o=jbossnotebook
member: uid=sam,ou=People,o=jbossnotebook
```

Make sure that your LDAP server is indexing the objectclass and member attributes. You'll need to search on them.

This data provides two primary entries, one for a user and one for a group, along with several structural entities to help keep the data organized. The user is a simple person object. We'll use the uid and userPassword attributes to indicate the user's name and password, respectively. The group is a groupOfNames object whose member attributes indicate who the group members are.

Although LDAP has standard-ized queries, there is no declarative way to express complex compound queries like you can with SQL.

Let's think through how we would authenticate and authorize a user from this data. Suppose the user sam enters his password, secretpassword. First, our login module would need to locate the entry for sam. This would require knowing that we should use the uid=sam entry under ou=People,dc=jboss,dc=org for the uid=sam entry. We can let the LDAP server take care of validating the user's credentials.

To find the roles for the user, we'd need to know to look for groups under ou=Roles,dc=jboss,dc=org. We'd also need to know to look for entries that contain member attributes whose value is the DN of the user's entry. Once we have those group names, we'd need to know how to map the DN of the role entry into a role name useful to JBoss.

Although your schema may be quite different, you'll need to follow the same thought process. If you can do that, you'll have no problem making your data work.

Now let's look at the configuration necessary to authenticate against an LDAP server that contains the data shown earlier. We'll need to use LdapLoginModule:

```
<application-policy name="todo">
    <authentication>
        <login-module code="org.jboss.security.auth.spi.LdapLoginModule"
                       flag="required">
            <module-option name="java.naming.factory.initial">
                com.sun.jndi.ldap.LdapCtxFactory
            </module-option>
            <module-option name="java.naming.provider.url">
                ldap://localhost/
            </module-option>
            <module-option name="java.naming.security.authentication">
                simple
            </module-option>
            <module-option name="principalDNPrefix">uid=</module-option>
            <module-option name="principalDNSuffix">
                ,ou=People,o=jbossnotebook
            </module-option>
            <module-option name="rolesCtxDN">
                ou=Roles,o=jbossnotebook
            </module-option>
            <module-option name="uidAttributeID">member</module-option>
            <module-option name="matchOnUserDN">true</module-option>
            <module-option name="roleAttributeID">cn</module-option>
            <module-option name="roleAttributeIsDN">false</module-option>
        </login-module>
    </authentication>
</application-policy>
```

There are a lot of options to configure, but the process isn't that tricky. The java.naming.* options are the JNDI properties to use to connect to the LDAP server. Notice that we are using simple authentication without specifying the DN and password of the user we want to connect as. The LDAP login module will attempt to connect as the user in question. It will construct a DN by prepending principalDNPrefix to the username and then appending the principalDNSuffix value.

rolesCtxDN provides the structural entity that holds the role entries. The uidAttributeID and matchOnUserDN values specify that we are searching for entries whose member attributes match the DN of the user we are trying to authenticate.

Finally, the roleAttributeID and roleAttributeIsDN values instruct the login module to use the cn attribute value of the role entry as the name of the role to assign to the user in JBoss. For the role object in our sample data, the cn attribute is JBossAdmin.

If you add the login module definition to your *login-config.xml* file, the application will start to authenticate against the user data you have in your LDAP server.

What about...

...more complex LDAP structures?

This is a very simplistic approach and it doesn't cover the many cases in which the DNs of your user entries don't fit such a neat and tidy pattern. Many LDAP servers use compound RDNs, or RDNs that don't make useful usernames. It's also common to have user information spread out over an entire subtree instead of neatly, one level below some root level. The LDAP login module doesn't address these complex cases. You would need to extend the login module to provide that functionality.

Stacking Login Modules

Sometimes no single login module meets your exact needs. Let's consider the case of using an external LDAP sever to provide user information. You would really consider this approach only if you needed to integrate with an existing LDAP-based user repository. But think about it for a second. Users and passwords map easily from a typical LDAP server, but how likely is it that the group and role information in an LDAP server will match up with the specific roles needed by your application? That rarely happens. To make matters worse, you might not be in control of the external LDAP server. It can be politically difficult to get your application-specific entries into the server.

That's not always the case, but it is certainly not uncommon to want to mix and match login modules. The case we just mentioned is a perfect example. You might have a user repository that lacks good role information. In that case, it would be nice to combine the LDAP login module validating users with the database login module providing role information.

How do I do that?

JBoss allows you to specify multiple login modules for a single security domain. It's like almost every other pluggable authentication system in that regard. The question is how the login modules interact. They can act cooperatively to authenticate the user, or they can work independently.

If you have multiple authentication repositories, you will want the authentication modules to work independently. Even if you have a companywide LDAP repository containing your users, you may need additional administrative user accounts that are specific to your application but that don't belong in your primary repository. A user would be in one repository or the other, and login should succeed if the user is found in either repository.

The following configuration accomplishes exactly that:

```
<application-policy name="todo">
    <authentication>
        <login-module code="org.jboss.security.auth.spi.LdapLoginModule"
                    flag="sufficient">
            <module-option name="java.naming.factory.initial">
                com.sun.jndi.ldap.LdapCtxFactory </module-option>
            <module-option name="java.naming.provider.url">
                ldap://localhost/
            </module-option>
            <module-option name="java.naming.security.authentication">
                simple
            </module-option>
            <module-option name="principalDNPrefix">uid= </module-option>
            <module-option name="principalDNSuffix">
                ,ou=People,o=jbossnotebook
            </module-option>
            <module-option name="rolesCtxDN">
                ou=Roles,o=jbossnotebook
            </module-option>
            <module-option name="uidAttributeID"> member </module-option>
            <module-option name="matchOnUserDN">true</module-option>
            <module-option name="roleAttributeID">cn</module-option>
            <module-option name="roleAttributeIsDN">false</module-option>
        </login-module>
        <login-module
            code="org.jboss.security.auth.spi.DatabaseServerLoginModule"
            flag="sufficient">
            <module-option name="dsJndiName">java:/DefaultDS</module-option>
            <module-option name="principalsQuery">
                select passwd from USERS where login=?
            </module-option>
            <module-option name="rolesQuery">
                select role, 'Roles' from USER_ROLES where login=?
            </module-option>
        </login-module>
    </authentication>
</application-policy>
```

Because we marked each module as sufficient, JBoss requires only one of the modules to succeed. If we left the modules marked required, JBoss would have required both modules to succeed, which would happen only if the user were in both repositories.

But what if the two repositories aren't independent? Going back to the original premise of having users in an LDAP server supplemented by application-specific roles in a relational database, simple module stacking doesn't solve the problem on its own. For that, you need to use password stacking.

Password stacking allows modules to skip the actual authentication and to provide supplemental roles, only if an earlier module has already authenticated the user. The modules require the `password-stacking` option to useFirstPass for this to work.

Here is an example:

```
<application-policy name="todo">
    <authentication>
        <login-module code="org.jboss.security.auth.spi.LdapLoginModule"
                    flag="required">
            <module-option name="password-stacking">
                useFirstPass</module-option>
            <module-option name="java.naming.factory.initial">
                com.sun.jndi.ldap.LdapCtxFactory </module-option>
            <module-option name="java.naming.provider.url">
                ldap://localhost/
            </module-option>
            <module-option name="java.naming.security.authentication">
                simple
            </module-option>
            <module-option name="principalDNPrefix">
                uid=
            </module-option>
            <module-option name="principalDNSuffix">
                ,ou=People,o=jbossnotebook
            </module-option>
        </login-module>
        <login-module
            code="org.jboss.security.auth.spi.DatabaseServerLoginModule"
            flag="required">
            <module-option
                name="password-stacking">useFirstPass</module-option>
            <module-option name="dsJndiName">java:/DefaultDS</module-option>
            <module-option name="rolesQuery">
                select role, 'Roles' from USER_ROLES where login=?
            </module-option>
        </login-module>
    </authentication>
</application-policy>
```

Both the LDAP login module and the database login module are marked required, and both have the `password-stacking` option set. Notice that the LDAP configuration omits the roles query information and the database server module omits the principals query. It is better to provide fallback queries even when they aren't used, but it isn't required.

What just happened?

You combined login modules to create more interesting authentication policies for your server. You can stack login modules to aggregate independent user repositories, or you can combine user repositories that provide partial information to create a complete policy for your application. The ability to combine login modules makes security configuration much more flexible.

Enabling SSL

Now we will shift gears and look at a completely different security issue. If you expect your applications to need secure HTTP communication, you'll need to enable SSL support.

How do I do that?

Before you can enable SSL, you will need to install a valid certificate on the server side. You can get one from a certification authority such as Thawte or VeriSign (and they come at a hefty price). Although you'll need a valid certificate before taking an application into production, For development purposes you can generate a certificate for your own use using the Java `keytool` command.

To generate a key, go to the *conf* directory of your server configuration and execute the following command:

```
[conf]$ keytool -genkey -keystore ssl.keystore -storepass mypassword \
-keypass mypassword -keyalg RSA -validity 3650  -alias testkey1 \
-dname "cn=testkey,o=jbossnotebook"
```

The key password should always be the same as the keystore password. If they are different, Tomcat won't be able to read the key.

This command produces a self-signed certificate. Self-signed certificates are signed only by the owner of the key (you), and not by a trusted certification authority. Since we aren't trying to generate a production certificate, you don't have to worry about the specifics of the type of key being generated. The important thing is that now you have an SSL-ready certificate in the *ssl.keystore* file.

To enable SSL, you'll need to point Tomcat to your keystore. This is quite simple to do. Just edit *deploy/jbossweb-tomcat55.sar/server.xml* and add the following connector:

```
<Connector port="8443" address="${jboss.bind.address}"
        maxThreads="100" strategy="ms" maxHttpHeaderSize="8192"
        emptySessionPath="true" scheme="https"
        secure="true" clientAuth="false"
        keystoreFile="${jboss.server.home.dir}/conf/ssl.keystore"
        keystorePass="mypassword" keyAlias="testkey1"
        sslProtocol="TLS" />
```

The keystore file, password, and alias should match the values you used when creating the keystore. After restarting JBoss, you should see the connector listening on port 8443 for HTTPS connections:

```
00:30:27,295 INFO  [Http11Protocol] Starting Coyote HTTP/1.1 on http-0.0.0.
0-8443
```

Now you can access the application securely using HTTPS on port 8443. To access the ToDo application, use *https://localhost:8443/todo/*.

Using a self-signed certificate leaves you vulnerable to the classic man-in-the-middle attack.

There is one small gotcha here, which you'll quickly notice when you try to access the application. Because the SSL certificate used wasn't signed by a trusted certification authority, your browser will complain that it can't verify the server's certificate. You can still communicate with the server over HTTPS, but you can't be certain that you are truly communicating with the server you think you are.

The solution is easy, but not free. It usually costs a good bit of money to get a certificate signed by a trusted certification authority. If you've generated a key using the keytool command, the first step is to generate a certificate signing request (CSR) to send to the certification authority. Here is how you generate a CSR with the keytool command:

```
[conf]$ keytool -certreq -keystore ssl.keystore -alias testkey1 \
-storepass mypassword -keypass mypassword  -keyalg RSA \
-file testreq.csr
```

You should send the *testreq.csr* file to your certification authority, along with a check covering the cost, at which point they'll respond with a signed certificate. If you save the certificate reply in a file called *cert.txt*, the following command will import it back into your keychain:

```
[conf]$ keytool -import -keystore ssl.keystore -alias testkey1 \
-storepass mypassword -keypass mypassword -file cert.txt

Top-level certificate in reply:

Owner: CN=Thawte Test CA Root, OU=TEST TEST TEST, O=Thawte Certification,
ST=FOR TESTING PURPOSES ONLY, C=ZA
Issuer: CN=Thawte Test CA Root, OU=TEST TEST TEST, O=Thawte Certification,
ST=FOR TESTING PURPOSES ONLY, C=ZA
Serial number: 0
Valid from: Wed Jul 31 19:00:00 CDT 1996 until: Thu Dec 31 15:59:59 CST 2020
Certificate fingerprints:
      MD5:  5E:E0:0E:1D:17:B7:CA:A5:7D:36:D6:02:DF:4D:26:A4
      SHA1: 39:C6:9D:27:AF:DC:EB:47:D6:33:36:6A:B2:05:F1:47:A9:B4:DA:EA
Certificate reply was installed in keystore
```

If your browser recognizes your chosen certification authority, you should be able to access your application over HTTPS without your web browser complaining that it can't validate the certificate.

CHAPTER 6

Logging

In this chapter, we are going to look at how JBoss handles logging. JBoss integrates the log4j logging framework as a core service of the application server. This means that JBoss provides not only extensive information about what the application server is doing at any given moment, but also the ability to centrally manage logging for all the applications in the server.

Centralizing log management has several nice benefits. It means that your applications don't need to worry about incompatible logging libraries. You also don't have to worry about application-specific logging configurations, or monitoring multiple application-specific logfiles. As a core JBoss service, you also gain the ability to dynamically reconfigure logging in a running server.

Let's get started and see what log4j can do.

Configuring log4j

The *log4j.xml* file in the *conf* directory controls all the logging for the server. This file has the definition of all the appenders that specify the logfiles, the categories of messages going to those logfiles, the layouts (formats) of those messages, and any filtering that will be done on those messages.

JBoss keeps two logs. The first is the core *server.log* file. The FILE appender provides the configuration:

```
<!-- A time/date based rolling appender -->
<appender name="FILE"
        class="org.jboss.logging.appender.DailyRollingFileAppender">
    <errorHandler class="org.jboss.logging.util.OnlyOnceErrorHandler"/>
```

For further information on log4j, see http://logging.apache.org.

```
        <param name="File" value="${jboss.server.home.dir}/log/server.log"/>
        <param name="Append" value="false"/>

        <!-- Rollover at midnight each day -->
        <param name="DatePattern" value="'.'yyyy-MM-dd"/>

        <layout class="org.apache.log4j.PatternLayout">
            <!-- The default pattern: Date Priority [Category] Message\n -->
            <param name="ConversionPattern" value="%d %-5p [%c] %m%n"/>
        </layout>
    </appender>
```

All log messages generated in the server are written to the *server.log* file. If you can't find the log message you are looking for, check this log. If the log message isn't in the *server.log* file, it isn't being generated. The appender used is DailyRollingFileAppender, which creates a new log-file each day. The *log4j.xml* file has an alternate configuration for the FILE appender that uses RollingFileAppender. That appender uses a size-based policy, rather than a date-based policy, to rotate logfiles. The alternative configuration is shown here:

```
<appender name="FILE"
          class="org.jboss.logging.appender.RollingFileAppender">
    <errorHandler class="org.jboss.logging.util.OnlyOnceErrorHandler"/>
    <param name="File" value="${jboss.server.home.dir}/log/server.log"/>
    <param name="Append" value="false"/>
    <param name="MaxFileSize" value="500KB"/>
    <param name="MaxBackupIndex" value="1"/>

    <layout class="org.apache.log4j.PatternLayout">
        <param name="ConversionPattern" value="%d %-5p [%c] %m%n"/>
    </layout>
</appender>
```

There are five basic levels of logging: DEBUG, INFO, WARN, ERROR, and FATAL. JBoss also has a special trace level that is used for fine-grained details of the server's operation.

The other log is the console log. When you run JBoss from the command line, as we have been doing, JBoss provides some basic logging information directly to the terminal window. This is actually the console log, and it is defined by the following appender definition:

```
<appender name="CONSOLE" class="org.apache.log4j.ConsoleAppender">
    <errorHandler class="org.jboss.logging.util.OnlyOnceErrorHandler"/>
    <param name="Target" value="System.out"/>
    <param name="Threshold" value="INFO"/>

    <layout class="org.apache.log4j.PatternLayout">
        <!-- The default pattern: Date Priority [Category] Message\n -->
        <param name="ConversionPattern"
               value="%d{ABSOLUTE} %-5p [%c{1}] %m%n"/>
    </layout>
</appender>
```

The big difference between the console log and *server.log* is that the console log has a threshold value of INFO. The console's threshold value limits the log messages to those with a level of INFO or higher. The console will contain INFO, WARN, and ERROR messages, but you won't see DEBUG messages there. You'll have to look in the *server.log* file to see those messages.

log4j.xml is the only file in the conf directory that JBoss pays attention to after startup.

If you want DEBUG messages to show up on the console, you need to change the Threshold value to DEBUG. Try changing the value while the server is running. You may have to wait for up to a minute for JBoss to notice the change, as it checks for changes to the *log4.xml* file every 60 seconds. When JBoss notices the change, it updates the logging configuration in memory and generates the following log message:

```
22:48:23,305 INFO  [Log4jService$URLWatchTimerTask] Configuring from
URL: resource:log4j.xml
```

Try undeploying or redepolying the ToDo application now. You'll notice that the console log displays much more in-depth information than it did before. If you get tired of the extra messages, set Threshold back to INFO. If you want even fewer messages on the console, try the WARN or ERROR level. WARN or ERROR is an appropriate threshold for a production server.

What just happened?

You found the global *log4j.xml* file and saw the configuration of the two core logfiles. You also changed the JBoss log level while it was running. JBoss monitors the *log4j.xml* file every 60 seconds.

Of course, you can customize the time between checks. By now, you should know enough about JBoss to guess that the log4j service is managed through a managed bean (MBean). You can find that MBean in the main *jboss-service.xml* file:

```
<mbean code="org.jboss.logging.Log4jService"
       name="jboss.system:type=Log4jService,service=Logging"
       xmbean-dd="resource:xmdesc/Log4jService-xmbean.xml">
    <attribute name="ConfigurationURL">resource:log4j.xml</attribute>
    <attribute name="Log4jQuietMode">true</attribute>
    <!-- How frequently in seconds the ConfigurationURL is checked for
         changes -->
    <attribute name="RefreshPeriod">60</attribute>
</mbean>
```

The RefreshPeriod attribute controls the time between checks. For development use, 5 or 10 seconds would be a more useful setting. Setting the value to a low value now will make the remaining labs go more quickly.

Adding a Logging Category

You've seen how appenders define logging destinations and filter log messages with a threshold. Now we will look at how to control the level of the log messages that are generated. Controlling the level of generated messages is important, both for performance and for keeping the *server.log* file from being flooded with messages that are more detailed than you need at any given time.

How do I do that?

All log messages are generated inside of named categories. Categories are hierarchical, allowing you to define appenders that cover a wide range of messages, and then turn around and define categories that target specific areas. The naming convention is similar to that used for Java classes and packages; category names are case-sensitive and use a dot as a separator. In fact, the standard convention is to name categories after the Java class or package in which they are being generated.

Here are a few categories from the *log4j.xml* file:

```
<!-- Limit the org.apache category to INFO as its DEBUG is verbose -->
<category name="org.apache">
    <priority value="INFO"/>
</category>

<!-- Limit the org.jgroups category to WARN as its INFO is verbose -->
<category name="org.jgroups">
    <priority value="WARN"/>
</category>

<!-- Limit apache axis to INFO as its DEBUG is even more verbose -->
<category name="org.jboss.axis">
    <priority value="INFO"/>
</category>
```

All generated log messages go to server.log. Individual category definitions are the only filter on that file.

These categories specify the minimum priority of messages that will be generated. The purpose of the categories is to limit the log messages produced by components to a level that makes sense. Although you can control the threshold on the appender, INFO messages on one component may be significantly more verbose than DEBUG messages on another. Filtering at the category level allows you to compensate for that disparity.

The ToDo application does some very basic logging in the beans using log4j. In TaskBean, for example, a log4j Logger instance is obtained using the name of the bean class as the category name:

```
import org.apache.log4j.Logger
// …
static Logger logger = Logger.getLogger(TaskBean.class);
```

The ejbCreate( ) method logs its activity using the debug( ) method on the logger instance:

```
/** @ejb.create-method */
public String ejbCreate(String user, String name)
    throws CreateException
{
    setId(TaskUtil.generateGUID(this));
    setName(name);
    setUser(user);
    setStartedDate(new Date());
    logger.debug("creating task " + getId( ) + " for user " + user);
    return null;
}
```

JBoss provides an extension to the log4j Logger class in org.jboss.logging. Logger. The JBoss Logger provides access to the trace-level logging extension used in the server for log statements more detailed than normal DEBUG logging.

When you access the application and create a task, the following statement gets logged to *server.log* showing the generated ID of the task being created:

```
2005-04-11 20:59:30,782 DEBUG [com.oreilly.jbossnotebook.todo.ejb.TaskBean]
creating task 3421f6bfc0a80064009b0b39004cf63c for user pinky
```

If you decide that you don't want EJB debug messages generated at all, you need to add a category for the component that limits the generated messages. The following category limits EJB debug messages to INFO:

```
<category name="com.oreilly.jbossnotebook.todo.ejb">
    <priority value="INFO" />
</category>
```

The message doesn't show up on the console since the threshold on the console is INFO.

Categories are hierarchical, and a category inherits its configuration from parent categories. You could also limit logging across the entire ToDo application by limiting a parent category:

```
<category name="com.oreilly.jbossnotebook.todo ">
    <priority value="INFO" />
</category>
```

The configuration on a category always takes precedence over the configuration on a parent category. It is possible to limit the application to INFO while allowing DEBUG messages from the EJB component, or to log the entire application at the DEBUG level while limiting only the EJBs to INFO, by providing configurations for both categories.

The inheritance chain goes all the way back to a special root category. The root category is configured using a root element. The JBoss-provided *log4j.xml* file contains a root element that looks like this:

```
<root>
    <appender-ref ref="CONSOLE" />
    <appender-ref ref="FILE" />
</root>
```

In this case, the root category doesn't declare a default priority. If you need a default log level for the entire server you can configure it there, but it is generally advisable to be more specific with categories.

Configuring the Log Format

If you look carefully at the *server.log* file and compare it to the messages output to the console, you'll notice that the formats are quite different. The log messages in *server.log* have a more precise time and show the fully qualified category name that the message is logged under. Each appender can declare the messages logged to it. We'll look at how to do that now.

How do I do that?

Each appender declares a layout to be used to output the log message using a `layout` element. Here is the normal configuration for the console log again:

```
<appender name="CONSOLE" class="org.apache.log4j.ConsoleAppender">
    <errorHandler class="org.jboss.logging.util.OnlyOnceErrorHandler"/>
    <param name="Target" value="System.out"/>
    <param name="Threshold" value="INFO"/>

    <layout class="org.apache.log4j.PatternLayout">
        <!-- The default pattern: Date Priority [Category] Message\n -->
        <param name="ConversionPattern"
               value="%d{ABSOLUTE} %-5p [%c{1}] %m%n"/>
    </layout>
</appender>
```

The `ConversionPattern` parameter controls the log format. We won't go into all the pattern options here. You can find full documentation of formatting options at *http://logging.apache.org/log4j/docs/api/org/apache/log4j/PatternLayout.html*.

Let's suppose you want to log the name of the thread that generated the log message. The pattern layout option for the thread name is %t. You just need to add that to `ConversionPattern` to make the change:

```
<param name="ConversionPattern" value="%d{ABSOLUTE} %-5p [%c{1}] (%t) %m%n"/>
```

After the change takes effect, the console log should begin logging messages like this:

```
00:26:37,856 INFO  [TaskBean] (http-0.0.0.0-8080-2:) Created:
local/Task@1735136:34df95cec0a8006500811ae4bccfc6e2
```

Creating a New Logfile

Having application logging handled by the server is very convenient, but mixing application and server logging can be confusing. You will probably want to create a separate logfile for each of your applications. This is quite easy to do in JBoss.

How do I do that?

Let's see how we can create a new logfile for the ToDo application. Appenders represent logging destinations, so creating a new logfile is as simple as creating a new appender. To make it easy, we'll use the FILE appender, which represents the *server.log* file, as a starting point:

```
<appender name="TODO"
          class="org.jboss.logging.appender.DailyRollingFileAppender">
    <errorHandler class="org.jboss.logging.util.OnlyOnceErrorHandler"/>
    <param name="File"        value="${jboss.server.home.dir}/log/todo.log"/>
    <param name="Append"      value="false"/>
    <param name="DatePattern" value="'.'yyyy-MM-dd"/>
    <layout class="org.apache.log4j.PatternLayout">
        <param name="ConversionPattern" value="%d %-5p [%c] %m%n"/>
    </layout>
</appender>
```

We've changed two things here: the logical name of the appender and the location of the logfile. The appender name is important because we need a way to refer to the appender later in the file, specifically to tell log4j which categories should be logged to this file. You may recall that the root category had two appender-ref elements on it that we didn't talk about. The appender-ref elements tell the category which appenders to send the generated log messages to:

```
<root>
    <appender-ref ref="CONSOLE"/>
    <appender-ref ref="FILE"/>
</root>
```

This tells log4j to send all messages to both the CONSOLE and FILE appenders. Nothing will be logged to our new *todo.log* file until we tell a category to send its messages there. To do that, add an appender-ref element to the category for the ToDo application:

```
<category name="com.oreilly.jbossnotebook.todo">
    <priority value="DEBUG" />
    <appender-ref ref="TODO"/>
</category>
```

At this point, you'll see a *todo.log* file created in the *log* directory. If you create a few tasks, the *server.log* file will start filling up with messages such as the following:

```
2005-04-12 09:50:50,366 DEBUG [com.oreilly.jbossnotebook.todo.ejb.TaskBean]
creating task 36e4227e7f00000100197971e1e97a97 for user pinky
2005-04-12 09:50:53,597 DEBUG [com.oreilly.jbossnotebook.todo.ejb.TaskBean]
creating task 36e42f1d7f000001005b6f0acf4c151c for user pinky
```

Creating a new logfile for the ToDo application doesn't stop the messages from being logged to the console or to *server.log* file if the threshold of the logfiles permits it.

What just happened?

You created a new logfile to capture application-specific logging information. Creating a new logfile is the easiest way to get the log messages you want in a place that is easy to monitor. You have complete control over the layout of the new file and can make sure that you get the information you want without affecting the primary logs.

You don't have to log messages just to files. The *log4j.xml* file contains examples of appenders that log messages to email, syslog servers, and even JMS queues. If you have priority log messages, you can even write an appender that sends the log messages out as SMS messages to your cell phone. With log4j, you have the flexibility to change the logging policy without having to change any of your code.

Rolling Logfiles

Messages get written to logfiles with no consideration for the files' size. If you didn't take some action to keep the size of the logfiles down, the files would grow and grow, eventually eating up all of your free disk space. To help solve this problem, JBoss provides the ability to periodically roll active logging over to a new logfile, leaving the old files around to be archived, or even deleted. There are two basic rotation policies: size-based and time-based. We've seen both of them in passing, but now we'll examine them in more detail.

How do I do that?

When specifying an appender, it is necessary to provide the name of the class that provides the actual implementation of the appender. We've already used DailyRollingFileAppender for *todo.log*:

```
<appender name="TODO"
          class="org.jboss.logging.appender.DailyRollingFileAppender">
    <errorHandler class="org.jboss.logging.util.OnlyOnceErrorHandler"/>
    <param name="File" value="${jboss.server.home.dir}/log/todo.log"/>
    <param name="Append" value="false"/>

    <!-- Rollover at midnight each day -->
    <param name="DatePattern" value="'.'yyyy-MM-dd"/>
    <layout class="org.apache.log4j.PatternLayout">
        <param name="ConversionPattern" value="%d %-5p [%c] %m%n"/>
    </layout>
</appender>
```

Logfiles are rolled only when there is activity. Don't expect to see logfiles rolling when your application is sitting idle.

DailyRollingFileAppender supports date-based rollover at these intervals: monthly, weekly, daily, twice a day at midnight and noon, and at the top of every hour and every minute. The DatePattern parameter controls both the frequency of the rollover and the name of the saved logfile. Because the date format uses the day as the lowest unit of time, a new logfile will be created nightly, with the old one archived to be renamed according to the date pattern: *todo.log-2005-04-04*, for example.

The other popular rolling strategy is to roll a new logfile only when the current one gets large. RollingFileAppender does this job:

```
<appender name="TODO"
          class="org.jboss.logging.appender.RollingFileAppender">
    <errorHandler class="org.jboss.logging.util.OnlyOnceErrorHandler"/>
    <param name="File"          value="${jboss.server.home.dir}/log/todo.log"/>
    <param name="Append"         value="false"/>
    <param name="MaxFileSize"      value="100KB"/>
    <param name="MaxBackupIndex" value="10"/>
    <layout class="org.apache.log4j.PatternLayout">
        <param name="ConversionPattern" value="%d %-5p [%c] %m%n"/>
    </layout>
</appender>
```

RollingFileAppender will create a new logfile when the size of the current log exceeds MaxFileSize. In this example, the maximum size is 100KB. The old logfiles will have an incremental index number added to the filename: *todo.log.1*, *todo.log.2*, etc. The older logs will have a higher index number. Log4j will keep MaxBackupIndex of old logfiles and will delete logfiles that are too old.

Adjusting Logging from the JMX Console

We've seen JBoss watch the *log4j.xml* file and reconfigure log4j when the file changes. That's not the only way to change log levels in the system. All services in JBoss are represented by MBeans that you can interact with remotely. The easiest way to do that is through the JMX Console application. We'll just touch on the JMX Console here, but in the next chapter we'll go much further into how it works. For now, let's see how we can adjust the logging level of a category.

How do I do that?

To get to the JMX Console you need to go to *http://localhost:8080/* in your browser. Click the JMX Console and find the jboss.system domain section. To access the log4j service, you should click on the service=Logging,type=Log4jService link. You'll see a list of MBean attributes and operations. You are looking for the getLoggerLevel operation, which looks like Figure 6-1.

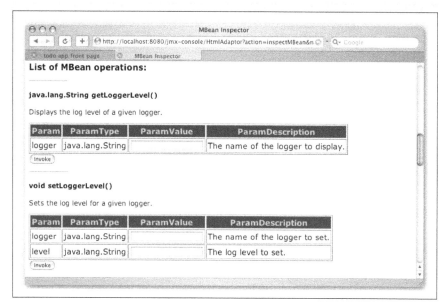

Figure 6-1. MBean operations for getLoggerLevel

The getLoggerLevel operation takes the name of a logging category and returns the level of that category. To see the log level for the com. oreilly.jbossnotebook.todo category, enter the category name and click the Invoke button. If you still have the category set to DEBUG or INFO, you will see that value returned. If you don't see any return value, you don't have the level set on the category.

The setLoggingLevel operation can adjust the log level of a category at runtime. Enter the same category and set the level parameter to ERROR. Don't worry if you don't see any output other than "Operation completed successfully without a return value." You can invoke the getLoggerLevel operation again to verify the level is correct. Checking the logfile is a great sanity check, too.

Setting log levels in the JMX Console doesn't modify log4j.xml. Changes made this way will be lost if the server resets, or the next time the log4j.xml file is loaded.

What just happened?

You used the JMX Console to get and set the log levels for the ToDo application. This is very useful when you have limited access to the application server machine. Going through the console can be easier than editing a configuration file on a remote machine. It's also useful when you want to temporarily play with log levels without changing the configuration state in *log4j.xml*.

HTTP Access Logs

Tomcat has support for logging, allowing you to track page-hit counts, user session activity, etc. Those logfiles are in the same format as those created by standard web servers. This allows you to use tools you may already have, to work with your web applications and to analyze how they're being used.

TIP

The standard HTTP logging format is at *http://www.w3.org/Daemon/ User/Config/Logging.html#common-logfile-format*.

How do I do that?

To enable HTTP logging, you need to go to the *deploy/jbossweb-tomcat55.sar* directory. There you will see the *server.xml* file, to which you'll need to add the following valve definition:

```
<Valve className="org.apache.catalina.valves.FastCommonAccessLogValve"
       prefix="localhost_access_log." suffix=".log"
       pattern="common" directory="${jboss.server.home.dir}/log"
       resolveHosts="false" />
```

You'll find the valve commented out, so all you really need to do is uncomment the definition. To get this to take effect you need to restart the JBoss server. Once you've restarted the server, Tomcat will create an access log, such as *localhost_access_log.2005-04-08.log*, where the date in your filename will be different. This file has the HTTP server requests logged into it, and in it you will see entries such as this:

```
127.0.0.1 - - [08/Apr/2005:05:21:55 -0600]
"GET /jmx-console/HtmlAdaptor? action=inspectMBean&name=jboss.system%3Aservice
%3DLogging%2Ctype%3DLog4jService HTTP/1.1" 200 10320
0:0:0:0:0:0:0:1 - - [08/Apr/2005:05:40:17 -0600]
"GET /todo/ HTTP/1.1" 401 952
0:0:0:0:0:0:0:1 - pinky [08/Apr/2005:05:40:23 -0600]
"GET /todo/ HTTP/1.1" 304 -
0:0:0:0:0:0:0:1 - pinky [08/Apr/2005:05:40:26 -0600]
"GET /todo/style.css HTTP/1.1" 304 -
0:0:0:0:0:0:0:1 - pinky [08/Apr/2005:05:40:26 -0600]
"GET /todo/front.faces HTTP/1.1" 200 11150
0:0:0:0:0:0:0:1 - pinky [08/Apr/2005:05:40:41 -0600]
"GET /todo/style.css HTTP/1.1" 304 -
0:0:0:0:0:0:0:1 - pinky [08/Apr/2005:05:40:41 -0600]
"POST /todo/front.faces HTTP/1.1" 200 1278
0:0:0:0:0:0:0:1 - pinky [08/Apr/2005:05:40:46 -0600]
"GET /todo/style.css HTTP/1.1" 304 -
0:0:0:0:0:0:0:1 - pinky [08/Apr/2005:05:40:46 -0600]
"POST /todo/task.faces HTTP/1.1" 200 1360
0:0:0:0:0:0:0:1 - pinky [08/Apr/2005:05:40:48 -0600]
"GET /todo/style.css HTTP/1.1" 304 -
0:0:0:0:0:0:0:1 - pinky [08/Apr/2005:05:40:48 -0600]
"POST /todo/task.faces HTTP/1.1" 200 11150
```

What just happened?

You enabled logging for the Tomcat web server that is built into JBoss. You restarted the server to get your changes to take effect. Then you went to different areas of JBoss and possibly your test application. Finally you looked into the logfile that is specific to the HTTP requests to see what it put in there.

One thing we didn't mention is that the logging format is the standard web request logging format, so it's easy to use these logfiles with products that support that. You can find more information about the Tomcat logging configuration at *http://jakarta.apache.org/tomcat/tomcat-5.5-doc/config/valve.html*.

Logging Generated SQL for CMP

So far we've seen ways to log from our domain objects and the web server. It would also be nice to see what was going on with the CMP layer of our application. The CMP layer takes care of our application's interaction with DB, and it can be very valuable to see what it is doing, and how. Let's see how to turn logging on for the CMP layer so that we can do just that.

How do I do that?

To turn on logging for the CMP, you need to add this category to your *log4j.xml* file:

```
<category name="org.jboss.ejb.plugins.cmp">
    <priority value="DEBUG"/>
</category>
```

You will also need to change the CONSOLE appender to have a Threshold of DEBUG:

```
<appender name="CONSOLE" class="org.apache.log4j.ConsoleAppender">
    <errorHandler class="org.jboss.logging.util.OnlyOnceErrorHandler"/>
    <param name="Target" value="System.out"/>
    <param name="Threshold" value="DEBUG"/>
    <layout class="org.apache.log4j.PatternLayout">
        <!-- The default pattern: Date Priority [Category] Message\n -->
        <param name="ConversionPattern"
                value="%d{ABSOLUTE} %-5p [%c{1}] %m%n"/>
    </layout>
</appender>
```

Now save the *log4j.xml* file and in about a minute your change will be applied. Once it is, add a new todo item or complete one you already have, and then look in the logfile. You should see something like this:

```
21:52:09,960 DEBUG [Task#findTasksForUser] Executing SQL: SELECT to_t.id
FROM TASK to_t WHERE (to_t.user = ?)
21:52:10,013 DEBUG [Task] Executing SQL: SELECT id, name, user, startedDate,
completedDate FROM TASK WHERE (id=?) OR (id=?) OR (id=?) OR (id=?) OR (id=?)
OR (id=?) OR (id=?)
21:52:10,072 DEBUG [Task] load relation SQL: SELECT task, id FROM COMMENT WHERE
(task=?) OR (task=?) OR (task=?) OR (task=?) OR (task=?) OR (task=?) OR (task=?)
21:52:20,003 INFO  [STDOUT] GENKEY!
21:52:20,198 DEBUG [TaskBean] creating task 962b26a9ac100a3800de002d994a5508
for user pinky
21:52:20,198 DEBUG [Task] Executing SQL: SELECT COUNT(*) FROM TASK WHERE id=?
21:52:20,205 DEBUG [Task] Executing SQL: INSERT INTO TASK (id, name, user,
startedDate, completedDate) VALUES (?, ?, ?, ?, ?)
21:52:20,222 INFO  [STDOUT] Created: local/Task@11157534:
962b26a9ac100a3800de002d994a5508
21:52:20,247 DEBUG [Task#findTasksForUser] Executing SQL: SELECT to_t.id FROM
TASK to_t WHERE (to_t.user = ?)
21:52:20,396 DEBUG [Task] Executing SQL: SELECT id, name, user, startedDate,
completedDate FROM TASK WHERE (id=?) OR (id=?) OR (id=?) OR (id=?) OR (id=?) OR
 (id=?) OR (id=?) OR (id=?)
21:52:20,403 DEBUG [Task] load relation SQL: SELECT task, id FROM COMMENT WHERE
(task=?) OR (task=?) OR (task=?) OR (task=?) OR (task=?) OR (task=?) OR (task=?)
OR (task=?)
```

```
21:52:20,537 DEBUG [Task#findTasksForUser] Executing SQL: SELECT t0_t.id FROM
TASK t0_t WHERE (t0_t.user = ?)
21:52:20,541 DEBUG [Task] Executing SQL: SELECT id, name, user, startedDate,
completedDate FROM TASK WHERE (id=?) OR (id=?) OR (id=?) OR (id=?) OR (id=?) OR
(id=?) OR (id=?) OR (id=?)
21:52:20,548 DEBUG [Task] load relation SQL: SELECT task, id FROM COMMENT
WHERE (task=?) OR (task=?) OR (task=?) OR (task=?) OR (task=?) OR (task=?)
OR (task=?) OR (task=?)
```

What just happened?

You enabled CMP logging by creating a category that the CMP layer will use. You also bumped up the logging target level to DEBUG. Then you waited for the server to detect those changes, and you saw some of the kinds of output you would get when your program interacts with the CMP.

What about...

...if you aren't seeing as much information regarding what the CMP layer is doing?

You can use the TRACE level of logging. You can enable it by modifying the category you created for CMP logging to look like this:

```
<category name="org.jboss.ejb.plugins.cmp">
    <priority value="TRACE" class="org.jboss.logging.XLevel"/>
</category>
```

This will allow the CMP layer to put out all the logging information that is configured in the code, even things such as developer tracing information. This may quickly generate a very big logging file due to how much information it will dump out.

And what about the commented out sections of log4j.xml?

One thing you probably noticed is that the appenders are mostly the same each time. You can usually create a new appender by copying an existing one and changing a few of the tags' values. The properties can stay the same most of the time. Another thing you may notice is that much of *log4j.xml* is commented out. As you learn more about JBoss you'll want to go back and examine these commented-out sections, as they provide preconfigured settings for SMTP logging, JMS logging, etc. To enable these features, in most cases you only need to remove the comment marks. There's a lot you can get logging information on. Be sure to read more of the online docs about logging, as they also have quite a bit more information.

CHAPTER 7

Configuring Persistence

The ToDo application is an EJB–based J2EE application, and JBoss deployed it with no container-specific configuration required. We've pulled back the curtains on the database layer and on security, and now it is time to pull back the curtains on the CMP entity beans and see how to customize their persistence.

Managing Schema

When you deployed the ToDo application, JBoss created the tables required by the entity beans. This is JBoss's default behavior, but JBoss can be even more helpful during the stages of development when your beans are more volatile and are undergoing constant change.

When your entity beans change, your database schema also has to change. It's great that JBoss creates the schema for you, but what happens when you need the schema to change? You could delete the tables from the database and redeploy the application to force JBoss to re-create the tables.

Fortunately, you don't need to do anything quite so heavy-handed. JBoss provides several options for schema management. We've seen automatic schema creation so far, but JBoss also provides automatic schema deletion and migration options, if you ask for them.

Keeping the database schema in sync with changing beans is always a huge drain on productivity.

How do I do that?

JBoss provides three schema management flags: `create-table`, `remove-table`, and `alter-table`. The `create-table` flag controls whether JBoss creates the required tables if they don't already exist when the application is deployed. The `remove-table` flag indicates whether JBoss should remove the tables for the application when the application is undeployed. Finally, the `alter-table` flag specifies whether JBoss should try to modify the table definition when the underlying bean changes.

You can set these three flags across the system, for a specific application, or for a specific entity bean or relation. The systemwide defaults are set in *standardjbosscmp-jdbc.xml* in the *conf* directory. If you look at the defaults section at the top of the file, you'll notice that `create-table` defaults to true, whereas `alter-table` and `remove-table` default to false.

It is generally not advisable to edit the systemwide configuration. If you want to change the schema policies, you can add the flags to your own *jbosscmp-jdbc.xml* file. You should place this deployment descriptor in the *META-INF* directory of an EJB jar file, alongside the *ejb-jar.xml* file.

You've already been operating with the `create-table` flag set to true, and you've seen JBoss create the database tables for you. Now we'll turn on the `remove-table` and `alter-table` flags. This change causes JBoss to remove the tables when it undeploys the application. It also causes JBoss to upgrade the schema should it find the tables already there.

That condition shouldn't occur if JBoss is removing the tables before undeploying the previous version of the application. However, the tables could exist if JBoss is stopped abruptly, perhaps due to a hardware or JVM failure, or if the previous version of the application doesn't have the remove-table flag set. The latter will be the case when you deploy the application for the first time with these flags set.

To set the flag, you'll need a *jbosscmp-jdbc.xml* file with all three flags set to true:

```
<!DOCTYPE jbosscmp-jdbc PUBLIC
        "-//JBoss//DTD JBOSSCMP-JDBC 4.0//EN"
        "http://www.jboss.org/j2ee/dtd/jbosscmp-jdbc_4_0.dtd">
<jbosscmp-jdbc>
    <defaults>
        <create-table>true</create-table>
        <alter-table>true</alter-table>
        <remove-table>true</remove-table>
    </defaults>
</jbosscmp-jdbc>
```

You'll find this file in the *etc/cmp* directory of the ToDo project. To make sure it is included in the deployed application, set the `optional.dd` flag to `cmp` when building:

```
[todo]$ ant -Doptional.dd=cmp main deploy
```

When you deploy the application, nothing interesting should happen. Since `remove-table` was `false` and there have been no schema changes,

This is a common JBoss configuration pattern. JBoss systemwide defaults can be overridden by application defaults, and application defaults can be overridden for each bean. You can choose whichever scope is most appropriate for your needs.

If you want to run the examples against a different database, make sure you set the database options that you saw in Chapter 4.

JBoss will simply redeploy the application, as we've seen it do many times already. However, once you do that, the `remove-table` flag will be true, and you'll see JBoss remove the tables when the application is undeployed.

To undeploy the application, you need to remove it from the *deploy* directory. The undeploy target in *build.xml* will do that:

```
[todo]$ ant undeploy
Buildfile: build.xml

undeploy:
    [delete] Deleting: /tmp/jboss-4.0.2/server/default/deploy/todo.ear
```

You can verify that JBoss removed the tables by launching the Hypersonic database manager and checking that the tables are indeed deleted. Or, if you still have CMP logging enabled, you can check the log messages to see the SQL statements issued.

If you redeploy the application, you'll see JBoss re-create the tables. That, of course, means that any tasks you had previously created are gone.

Now we'll explore the table modification capabilities. For that, you'll need to turn off `remove-table`. Edit *jbosscmp-jdbc.xml* as shown here:

```
<!DOCTYPE jbosscmp-jdbc PUBLIC
          "-//JBoss//DTD JBOSSCMP-JDBC 4.0//EN"
          "http://www.jboss.org/j2ee/dtd/jbosscmp-jdbc_4_0.dtd">
<jbosscmp-jdbc>
    <defaults>
        <create-table>true</create-table>
        <alter-table>true</alter-table>
        <remove-table>false</remove-table>
    </defaults>
</jbosscmp-jdbc>
```

Redeploy the application to make sure that it is in a state where the tables won't be removed. It will also be helpful to add some tasks in the application to see that your data is preserved, even through schema updates.

To change to the schema, we'll add a priority field to TaskBean. Doing that is quite painless. You'll need to add the following abstract getter and setter methods, with the appropriate XDoclet attributes, to *TaskBean. java*:

```
/**
 * @ejb.persistence
 * @ejb.interface-method
 */
public abstract int getPriority();
```

The biggest drawback to removing the tables is that you will lose any data you had created. If your application requires seed data, you'll have to remember to populate the database again.

```
/** @ejb.interface-method */
public abstract void setPriority(int priority);
```

Build and deploy the application again, just as you did earlier:

```
[todo]$ ant -Doptional.dd=cmp main deploy
```

JBoss has added a new `priority` column to the TASK table. You can verify it through the database manager. If you still have it running, you'll
need to refresh the schema view by selecting Refresh Tree from the View
menu. Schema updates are logged at the WARN level, so you will see a
notice of the change in the console log:

```
16:44:44,765 WARN  [Task] ALTER TABLE TASK ADD COLUMN priority INTEGER NOT
NULL
```

For illustrative purposes, you can remove the `getPriority` and
`setPriority` methods from `TaskBean`, returning it to its original state, and
redeploy the application again. This time JBoss will notice that the field
is missing and will remove the `priority` column:

```
16:46:57,339 WARN  [Task] ALTER TABLE TASK DROP COLUMN PRIORITY
```

What just happened?

JBoss is able to help you not only rapidly deploy J2EE applications, but
also keep up with rapid changes in your application. When JBoss was
combined with XDoclet, you were able to add a persistent field to an
entity bean in about 30 seconds. The database schema was updated,
and the value object code was changed, making the field immediately
accessible to the web tier.

Mapping Objects

The generated schema is nice for development, but at some point, you'll
reach the stage where you want to customize the schema to conform to
your naming or datatype needs. Or perhaps your DBA will prefer to take
over and provide schema optimized for your database. In that case, you'll
need JBoss to play nicely with your schema. In this lab, you'll see how to
control table names, field names and type mapping details

How do I do that?

We'll start by looking more closely at the schema JBoss created. JBoss
created a table for each entity bean:

```
CREATE TABLE TASK
(
```

```
        id VARCHAR(256) NOT NULL,
        name VARCHAR(256),
        user VARCHAR(256),
        startedDate TIMESTAMP,
        completedDate TIMESTAMP,
        CONSTRAINT PK_TASK PRIMARY KEY (id)
    )

    CREATE TABLE COMMENT
    (
        id VARCHAR(256) NOT NULL,
        commentText VARCHAR(256),
        date TIMESTAMP,
        task VARCHAR(256),
        CONSTRAINT PK_COMMENT PRIMARY KEY (id)
    )
```

The table names come from the ejb-name name of the beans, and the column names are the field names of persistent fields on the beans. We'll want to update the names to use more normal database conventions.

JBoss will select different names when the table or column name is a common SQL reserved word. The full list of reserved words comes from standardjboss-cmp-jdbc.xml.

The type information is slightly more complex. Each supported database has a type-mapping section in the *standardjbosscmp-jdbc.xml* file that contains mappings from Java classes to JDBC and SQL types. The task and comment beans use only two basic types: java.lang.String and java.util.Date. Here are the mappings for those two types:

```
<type-mapping>
    <name>Hypersonic SQL</name>
    <!-- … lots of other types deleted … -->
    <mapping>
        <java-type>java.lang.String</java-type>
        <jdbc-type>VARCHAR</jdbc-type>
        <sql-type>VARCHAR(256)</sql-type>
    </mapping>
    <mapping>
        <java-type>java.util.Date</java-type>
        <jdbc-type>TIMESTAMP</jdbc-type>
        <sql-type>TIMESTAMP</sql-type>
    </mapping>
</type-mapping>
```

The default date mapping differs by database. It's better to use java.sql.Date, java.sql.Time, and java.sql.Timestamp rather than java.util.Date to avoid any mapping confusion.

That explains where the type mapping for each column comes from. These mappings make sense as defaults, but it's easy to imagine wanting to use different values for specific fields.

The date mapping looks fine for our needs, since the intention is to provide a date and time value. However, the string values could use some tweaking. The task name and comment lengths of 256 characters are probably OK for now, but the UUID primary key values will always be 32 characters in length. You can change the type when you are updating the table and column names.

To make these changes, you'll need to go back to the *jbosscmp-jdbc.xml* file. After the `defaults` section, you can have an `enterprise-beans` section that contains the CMP configuration for each of your entity beans:

```
<jbosscmp-jdbc>
    <enterprise-beans>
        <entity>
            <ejb-name>Task</ejb-name>
            <!-- configuration for the task bean -->
        </entity>
        <entity>
            <ejb-name>Comment</ejb-name>
            <!-- configuration for the comment bean -->
        </entity>
    </enterprise-beans>
</jbosscmp-jdbc>
```

The structure of this element resembles that of the `enterprise-beans` element in an *ejb-jar.xml* file, with an `entity` section for each bean. This similarity is intentional. The `ejb-name` element links the entity to an entity with the same `ejb-name` in the neighboring *ejb-jar.xml* file.

The naming scheme here is completely arbitrary. The point is that you can choose any naming policy that makes sense for your application.

The first thing you can configure is the table name that the entity maps to. The `table-name` element specifies the name of the table to use:

```
<entity>
    <ejb-name>Task</ejb-name>
    <table-name>TODO_TASK</table-name>
</entity>
```

We've chosen to add the suffix TODO_ to the name of the bean to make it easier to group the tables related to the ToDo application.

You can add a `cmp-field` element for each regular CMP field you want to map. The `field-name` element links this element to a named `cmp-field` element in the *ejb-jar.xml* file, and the `column-name` element specifies the name of the column that the field maps to. Here is a mapping for the id field of TaskBean:

```
<cmp-field>
    <field-name>id</field-name>
    <column-name>TASK_ID</column-name>
</cmp-field>
```

You've already seen that JBoss maps this field to VARCHAR(256) in the database because it is a String field. However, the primary keys used by the application are always 32-character UUIDs. So, we'd really rather have this field converted to VARCHAR(32) in the database.

You can provide an override to the jdbc-type and sql-type elements you saw in the default mappings in *standardjbosscmp-jdbc.xml*. Now the complete configuration looks like this:

```
<cmp-field>
    <field-name>id</field-name>
    <column-name>TASK_ID</column-name>
    <jdbc-type>VARCHAR</jdbc-type>
    <sql-type>VARCHAR(32)</sql-type>
</cmp-field>
```

jdbc-type and sql-type always go together. You can't specify one without the other.

When overriding types in this manner, be aware that you lose database independence. Normally, changing databases would cause a new, and potentially different, type mapping to be loaded from *standardjbosscmp-jdbc.xml*. However, when overriding types in this manner, the type remains constant regardless of the database in use. It's not much of a limitation, but it is something to keep in mind if you are designing an application that will be deployed on multiple databases.

There's nothing tricky in mapping the rest of the fields. The complete *jbosscmp-jdbc.xml* file is shown here:

```
<!DOCTYPE jbosscmp-jdbc PUBLIC
        "-//JBoss//DTD JBOSSCMP-JDBC 4.0//EN"
        "http://www.jboss.org/j2ee/dtd/jbosscmp-jdbc_4_0.dtd">
<jbosscmp-jdbc>
    <defaults>
        <create-table>true</create-table>
        <alter-table>true</alter-table>
        <remove-table>false</remove-table>
    </defaults>
    <enterprise-beans>
        <entity>
            <ejb-name>Task</ejb-name>
            <table-name>TODO_TASK</table-name>
            <cmp-field>
                <field-name>id</field-name>
                <column-name>TASK_ID</column-name>
                <jdbc-type>VARCHAR</jdbc-type>
                <sql-type>VARCHAR(32)</sql-type>
            </cmp-field>
            <cmp-field>
                <field-name>name</field-name>
                <column-name>TASK_NAME</column-name>
            </cmp-field>
            <cmp-field>
                <field-name>user</field-name>
                <column-name>TASK_USER</column-name>
            </cmp-field>
            <cmp-field>
                <field-name>startedDate</field-name>
                <column-name>TASK_START</column-name>
            </cmp-field>
            <cmp-field>
                <field-name>completedDate</field-name>
                <column-name>TASK_END</column-name>
            </cmp-field>
```

```
        </entity>
        <entity>
            <ejb-name>Comment</ejb-name>
            <table-name>TODO_COMMENT</table-name>
            <cmp-field>
                <field-name>id</field-name>
                <column-name>COMMENT_ID</column-name>
                <jdbc-type>VARCHAR</jdbc-type>
                <sql-type>VARCHAR(32)</sql-type>
            </cmp-field>
            <cmp-field>
                <field-name>commentText</field-name>
                <column-name>COMMENT_TEXT</column-name>
            </cmp-field>
            <cmp-field>
                <field-name>date</field-name>
                <column-name>COMMENT_DATE</column-name>
            </cmp-field>
        </entity>
    </enterprise-beans>
</jbosscmp-jdbc>
```

This is included in the *etc/cmp-field* directory, and you can deploy it from the build file by setting `optional.dd` to `cmp-field`:

```
[todo]$ ant -Doptional.dd=cmp-field main deploy
```

When you do this, JBoss creates the following schema:

```
CREATE TABLE TODO_TASK
(
    TASK_ID VARCHAR(32) NOT NULL,
    TASK_NAME VARCHAR(256),
    TASK_USER VARCHAR(256),
    TASK_START TIMESTAMP,
    TASK_END TIMESTAMP,
    CONSTRAINT PK_TODO_TASK PRIMARY KEY (TASK_ID)
)

CREATE TABLE TODO_COMMENT
(
    COMMENT_ID VARCHAR(32) NOT NULL,
    COMMENT_TEXT VARCHAR(256),
    COMMENT_DATE TIMESTAMP,
    task VARCHAR(32),
    CONSTRAINT PK_TODO_COMMENT PRIMARY KEY (COMMENT_ID)
)
```

The task column on TODO_ COMMENT is a CMR field, not a CMP field. We'll set to CMR fields shortly.

What just happened?

You learned how JBoss maps entity beans. You saw the default naming strategy and saw the default type mappings in *standardjbosscmp-jdbc.xml*. You customized the basic CMP mapping of the entity beans, overriding both the name and the type of the default mappings in the *jbosscmp-jdbc.* *xml* deployment descriptor.

JBoss created the new schema for you when you deployed the application. If you didn't have the `remove-table` flag set to delete the old tables on undeployment, you'd still have the original TASK and COMMENT tables alongside the new TODO_TASK and TODO_COMMENT. This is true although `alter-table` was `true`.

JBoss had no way of knowing that the TASK table was actually the old TODO_TASK table when it deployed the application. As far as it's concerned, TASK could be a completely different and unrelated table. JBoss won't drop the old table or attempt to rename it. It's a manual step.

Nothing went wrong here, but something very well could have. Try changing the type of one of the ID fields from VARCHAR(32) back to VARCHAR(256) and redeploy the application. Did JBoss change your schema? It didn't, at least not if you are still working with Hypersonic. Hypersonic can't alter the type of a column. It's just a limitation of the database that JBoss can't work around.

Even if you are working with another database that supports altering types, JBoss will actually attempt to change only the types of CHAR or VARCHAR fields, and then only if the new field is longer in length than the old field. It's certainly limiting, but there are fundamental limitations in what can be done programmatically. At some point human intervention is required.

Mapping Relations

You aren't done with the mapping. You've mapped the entity beans to the field level, but you haven't touched the container-managed relationship yet. In the ToDo application, tasks have a one-to-many relationship with comments that needs to be captured in the schema.

Actually, the relationship was captured. The comment bean has a field named `task` that contains the ID of the task that it is related to. JBoss even figured out that it needed to change the type of the foreign key to VARCHAR(32) when you changed the type of the primary key fields, but it didn't conform to the naming conventions we used. You'll fix that. You'll also see that this isn't the only option for managing the relationship. Even though it's not strictly necessary for a one-to-many relationship, you'll see how to manage the relationship with a separate middle table.

How do I do that?

Let's get some terminology out of the way. There are three types of object relationships: one-to-one, one-to-many, and many-to-many. The distinction lies in the multiplicity of both sides of a relationship.

The task-comment relationship is a one-to-many relationship because every task can have many comments, but each comment belongs to only one task. If each task could have only a single comment associated with it, it would be a one-to-one relationship. On the other hand, if the same comment could be attached to multiple tasks (not just the same comment text, but the same comment object) that would be a many-to-many relationship.

If either side of the relationship is a "one" relationship, meaning that it is related to only one object on the other side of the relationship, you can use a foreign key mapping. JBoss used a foreign key mapping to relate a comment to its associated tasks. The primary key of the task to which the comment belongs is stored with the comment.

JBoss gave us a simple mapping by default. To customize it, you'll need to go back to the *jbosscmp-jdbc.xml* file and add a relationships element that again mirrors the relationships element in the *ejb-jar.xml* file. It contains an ejb-relation for each relation you want to configure, and the ejb-relation-name matches up a relation in *jbosscmp-jdbc.xml* with one in *ejb-jar.xml*. The structure looks like this:

```
<!DOCTYPE jbosscmp-jdbc PUBLIC
        "-//JBoss//DTD JBOSSCMP-JDBC 4.0//EN"
        "http://www.jboss.org/j2ee/dtd/jbosscmp-jdbc_4_0.dtd">
<jbosscmp-jdbc>
    <defaults>
        <!-- … -->
    </defaults>
    <enterprise-beans>
        <!-- … -->
    </enterprise-beans>
    <relationships>
        <ejb-relation>
            <ejb-relation-name>task-comment</ejb-relation-name>
            <!-- details on the relationship -->
        </ejb-relation>
    </relationships>
</jbosscmp-jdbc>
```

To declare the relationship as a foreign key mapping, add a foreign-key-mapping element to ejb-relation:

```
<ejb-relation>
    <ejb-relation-name>task-comment</ejb-relation-name>
    <foreign-key-mapping/>
    <!-- details on the relationship -->
</ejb-relation>
```

Each ejb-relation has two named roles, representing both sides of the relationship. The ejb-relationship-role-name links an ejb-relationship-role in *jbosscmp-jdbc.xml* to an ejb-relationship-role in *ejb-jar.xml*.

```
<ejb-relation>
    <ejb-relation-name>task-comment</ejb-relation-name>
    <foreign-key-mapping/>
    <ejb-relationship-role>
        <ejb-relationship-role-name>
            comment-belongs-to-task
        </ejb-relationship-role-name>
        <!-- configuration for the relationship role -->
    </ejb-relationship-role>
    <ejb-relationship-role>
        <ejb-relationship-role-name>
            task-has-comments
        </ejb-relationship-role-name>
        <!-- configuration for the relationship role -->
    </ejb-relationship-role>
</ejb-relation>
```

If you've ever wondered why each side of a relationship needs to be named, this is why. The sides have to be named so that you can apply additional external configurations to them.

The final step is to add a key-fields element on the task-has-comments relationship role to specify the column name of the foreign key field:

```
<ejb-relationship-role>
    <ejb-relationship-role-name>
        task-has-comments
    </ejb-relationship-role-name>
    <key-fields>
        <key-field>
            <field-name>id</field-name>
            <column-name>TASK_ID</column-name>
        </key-field>
    </key-fields>
</ejb-relationship-role>
</ejb-relationship-role>
```

The TASK_ID column goes on the table for the comment bean, so it may seem odd to associate it with the task side of the relationship in this way. In JBoss, key fields for relationships are always defined on the source side of the relationship, regardless of whether they are mapped as foreign keys in another entity table or in a middle table. Although it may seem slightly odd in this particular case, JBoss is very consistent.

The complete configuration looks like this:

```
<!DOCTYPE jbosscmp-jdbc PUBLIC
        "-//JBoss//DTD JBOSSCMP-JDBC 4.0//EN"
        "http://www.jboss.org/j2ee/dtd/jbosscmp-jdbc_4_0.dtd">
<jbosscmp-jdbc>
    <defaults>
        <!-- … -->
    </defaults>
```

```
<enterprise-beans>
    <!-- … -->
</enterprise-beans>
<relationships>
    <ejb-relation>
        <ejb-relation-name>task-comment</ejb-relation-name>
        <foreign-key-mapping/>
        <ejb-relationship-role>
            <ejb-relationship-role-name>
                comment-belongs-to-task
            </ejb-relationship-role-name>
        </ejb-relationship-role>
        <ejb-relationship-role>
            <ejb-relationship-role-name>
                task-has-comments
            </ejb-relationship-role-name>
            <key-fields>
                <key-field>
                    <field-name>id</field-name>
                    <column-name>TASK_ID</column-name>
                </key-field>
            </key-fields>
        </ejb-relationship-role>
    </ejb-relation>
</relationships>
</jbosscmp-jdbc>
```

To deploy this configuration, set `optional.dd` to `cmr-fk` and build the application:

```
[todo]$ ant -Doptional.dd=cmr-fk main deploy
```

When you do that, JBoss will update the table to look like this:

```
CREATE TABLE TODO_COMMENT
(
    COMMENT_ID VARCHAR(32) NOT NULL,
    COMMENT_TEXT VARCHAR(256),
    COMMENT_DATE TIMESTAMP,
    TASK_ID VARCHAR(32),
    CONSTRAINT PK_TODO_COMMENT PRIMARY KEY (COMMENT_ID)
)
```

This is most likely the way you will want to approach one-to-many relationships, but you might also want to use a middle table to map tasks to comments. Middle tables are generally reserved for many-to-many relationships in which neither side has a *one* relationship to which to attach a foreign key. However, you never know what type of relational mappings you may need in the field, and since middle tables are configured exactly the same way regardless of the multiplicity of the relationship, it will be a good example.

To do that, the foreign-key-mapping element needs to be replaced with a relation-table-mapping element that contains the name of the middle table:

```
<ejb-relation>
    <ejb-relation-name>task-comment</ejb-relation-name>
    <relation-table-mapping>
        <table-name>TODO_TASK_COMMENT</table-name>
    </relation-table-mapping>
    <!--relationship roles -->
</ejb-relation>
```

The middle table needs to have a foreign key reference for each side of the relationship, so both sides need to declare a complete key-fields element for their respective keys. The complete ejb-relation looks like this:

```
<ejb-relation>
    <ejb-relation-name>task-comment</ejb-relation-name>
    <relation-table-mapping>
        <table-name>TODO_TASK_COMMENT</table-name>
    </relation-table-mapping>
    <ejb-relationship-role>
        <ejb-relationship-role-name>
            comment-belongs-to-task
        </ejb-relationship-role-name>
        <key-fields>
            <key-field>
                <field-name>id</field-name>
                <column-name>COMMENT_ID</column-name>
            </key-field>
        </key-fields>
    </ejb-relationship-role>
    <ejb-relationship-role>
        <ejb-relationship-role-name>
            task-has-comments
        </ejb-relationship-role-name>
        <key-fields>
            <key-field>
                <field-name>id</field-name>
                <column-name>TASK_ID</column-name>
            </key-field>
        </key-fields>
    </ejb-relationship-role>
</ejb-relation>
```

The complete *jbosscmp-jdbc.xml* file for this configuration is available in the *etc/cmr-table* directory and you can deploy it by setting optional.dd to cmr-table when building:

```
[todo]$ ant -Doptional.dd=cmr-table main deploy
```

It really isn't far-fetched at all. You might not always be able to add relationship fields to an existing table just to satisfy the needs of your application.

When you deploy, the TODO_COMMENT table will no longer contain a foreign key field. In its place, JBoss creates the TODO_TASK_COMMENT table as instructed:

```
CREATE TABLE TODO_TASK_COMMENT
(
    COMMENT_ID VARCHAR(32) NOT NULL,
    TASK_ID VARCHAR(32) NOT NULL,
    CONSTRAINT PK_TODO_TASK_COMMENT PRIMARY KEY (COMMENT_ID, TASK_ID)
)
```

What just happened?

You completed the object-relational mapping configuration for the beans. You saw both basic foreign key mapping as well as relational table mapping with a middle table. While the entity beans in the ToDo application demonstrate only a one-to-many relationship, the configuration is exactly the same regardless of the multiplicity of the relationships.

What about...

...using XDoclet to generate the mapping details?

XDoclet does indeed have code generation tasks that will generate the JBoss deployment descriptors, just as it generates the J2EE deployment descriptors. We've chosen not to use them here because the prime directive of code generation is to never generate things that you don't understand. While you are still learning about the JBoss deployment descriptors, it is better to code them by hand. After you have mastered them, you can come back and add the appropriate XDoclet tags to allow all of this work to be done behind the scenes.

Adding Audit Data

It's often not enough to simply store data in a relational database. Many applications need to keep information about who created each row, and when. Often, it is also necessary to know who last edited the data, and when. This type of data is referred to as *audit data*.

Audit data is a common requirement for enterprise applications. While it is possible to build audit data into your application, it is easier to let JBoss manage the audit data for you. JBoss can track the creation and modification of entity beans as additional persistent data. This data can exist only in the database to be used for administrative purposes, or you can map it onto persistent fields in your entity beans to be used by the application.

How do I do that?

Since all access to the entity beans is managed by the application server, JBoss should be able to easily track who is editing the bean data and when they are doing it. We say *should* because, as the application stands now, JBoss isn't enforcing any security on the EJB tier.

When you configured the security policy in Chapter 5, you were only concerned about security into the web application. The beans are local EJBs with no remote view, so there is no need to worry about protecting them from access. J2EE role–based security is too primitive to do anything interesting at the EJB tier anyway, so we ignored the fact that we didn't have any security configuration on the EJB tier.

Fortunately, JBoss isn't limited to J2EE security. JBoss allows you to replace the simple method permission checks with much more interesting policies.

When you enable audit information, user information has to come into the EJB tier from the web tier to provide the user portion of the audit information. For that, you need a proper security domain linked to the application.

On the web tier, you linked to a security domain by adding a security-domain element to *jboss-web.xml*. On the EJB side, you need to add the same security-domain element to your *jboss.xml* file:

```
<!DOCTYPE jboss PUBLIC
        "-//JBoss//DTD JBOSS 4.0//EN"
        "http://www.jboss.org/j2ee/dtd/jboss_4_0.dtd">
<jboss>
    <security-domain>java:/jaas/todo</security-domain>
</jboss>
```

Since the security domain is the same, java:/jaas/todo, JBoss will pass user information seamlessly from the web tier into the EJB tier. We've already declared all the bean methods as unchecked, so JBoss won't restrict access to the beans in any way. However, information about the current authenticated user is now available to the audit fields.

Four audit fields are available: created-by, created-time, updated-by, and updated-time. These correspond to the user and time information related to when the bean was created and the last time it was updated. You can enable each audit field by providing the corresponding element inside the audit element for an entity in *jbosscmp-jdbc.xml*.

JBoss configuration files should make enough sense by now that we can just jump to a complete example. For each audit field, you need to add a column-name element that supplies the column name in which JBoss should write the audit data. The following configuration adds all four audit fields to the task bean:

```
<entity>
    <ejb-name>Task</ejb-name>
    <table-name>TODO_TASK</table-name>
    <!-- cmp-field -->
    <audit>
        <created-by>
            <column-name>AUDIT_CREATED_BY</column-name>
        </created-by>
        <created-time>
            <column-name>AUDIT_CREATED_TIME</column-name>
        </created-time>
        <updated-by>
            <column-name>AUDIT_UPDATED_BY</column-name>
        </updated-by>
        <updated-time>
            <column-name>AUDIT_UPDATED_TIME</column-name>
        </updated-time>
    </audit>
</entity>
```

The complete file is available in *etc/audit/jbosscmp-jdbc.xml*. You can add this file to the application by setting optional.dd to audit when building:

```
[todo]$ ant -Doptional.dd=audit main deploy
```

When you do this, JBoss will create the following table:

```
CREATE TABLE TODO_TASK
(
    TASK_ID VARCHAR(32) NOT NULL,
    TASK_NAME VARCHAR(256),
    TASK_USER VARCHAR(256),
    TASK_START TIMESTAMP,
    TASK_END TIMESTAMP,
    AUDIT_CREATED_BY VARCHAR(256) NOT NULL,
    AUDIT_CREATED_TIME TIMESTAMP NOT NULL,
    AUDIT_UPDATED_BY VARCHAR(256) NOT NULL,
    AUDIT_UPDATED_TIME TIMESTAMP NOT NULL,
    CONSTRAINT PK_TODO_TASK PRIMARY KEY (TASK_ID)
)
```

If the type isn't to your liking, you can override type information for an audit field by specifying JDBC and SQL types, just as you can for CMP fields:

```
<created-by>
    <column-name>AUDIT_CREATED_BY</column-name>
    <jdbc-type>VARCHAR</jdbc-type>
    <sql-type>VARCHAR(40)</sql-type>
</created-by>
```

These audit fields are stored in the database. You can use them in administrative tools, but the data isn't available to the application. That's a shame in terms of the ToDo application because the AUDIT_CREATED_BY and AUDIT_CREATED_TIME fields are, for all practical purposes, copies of the TASK_USER and TASK_STARTED fields. It would simplify the application a bit if we could merge the redundant columns and let JBoss populate the fields on object creation.

To do that, you need to replace the column-name element in the audit fields with a field-name element that links the audit field with an existing CMP field in the application:

It is more likely that you would simply add new CMP fields and map the audit data to them.

```
<audit>
    <created-by>
        <field-name>user</field-name>
    </created-by>
    <created-time>
        <field-name>startedDate</field-name>
    </created-time>
</audit>
```

With this configuration, the schema reverts to its previous form without the separate audit fields:

```
CREATE TABLE TODO_TASK
(
    TASK_ID VARCHAR(32) NOT NULL,
    TASK_NAME VARCHAR(256),
    TASK_USER VARCHAR(256),
    TASK_START TIMESTAMP,
    TASK_END TIMESTAMP,
    CONSTRAINT PK_TODO_TASK PRIMARY KEY (TASK_ID)
)
```

Here's how this works: if the application doesn't specify user or startedDate values when a bean instance is created, JBoss will populate the field with the appropriate audit information. The application obviously is doing this in the ejbCreate method of TaskBean, but it's easy enough to take that code out. The lines to remove are shown commented out in the following code:

```
/** @ejb.create-method */
public String ejbCreate(String user, String name)
    throws CreateException
{
    setId(TaskUtil.generateGUID(this));
    setName(name);
    // setUser(user);
    // setStartedDate(new Date());
    logger.debug("creating task " + getId() + " for user " + user);
    return null;
}
```

If you make these changes and redeploy the application, you will find that JBoss will populate values exactly as expected.

What just happened?

You saw how to add audit information for any CMP entity bean. Audit fields work exactly like regular CMP fields, and you have control over both the name and the type of field. If you prefer to integrate the audit information into the bean itself, you can map the audit information onto any CMP field on the bean.

Generating Primary Keys

Many projects add a key-generated session bean for this, but it is much nicer if you can use a transparent service provided by the application server.

The ToDo application uses UUID-like primary keys created by code that XDoclet generated. We chose this method because it was an easy and portable method of generating primary keys without any dependencies on JBoss. As you've seen, it works fine, but there are many other options besides pseudo-UUIDs.

We easily could have chosen another method, such as sequence tables or auto-increment columns on the database. There are many possibilities, but they all require extra code to be written, code that potentially has hard dependencies on the database type. We would prefer to keep that code outside of the application, if possible.

JBoss provides a way to attach a primary key generator to an entity bean to do exactly that. The bean can completely ignore primary key generation and leave the key generation policy as a deployment-time configuration option.

How do I do that?

When we wrote the ToDo application, we decided to use UUID strings as key objects. That's an acceptable decision, especially considering our goal to create an application that can be deployed with no external configuration, but it limits the key generation options. Most key generation strategies use numeric keys instead of string-based keys. Instead of limiting the discussion to text keys, we are going to rewrite the application to use numeric primary keys.

This rewrite is not as big as you might expect, since XDoclet manages most of the EJB tier for you. You need to change the id fields to be of type Integer, like this:

```
/**
 * @ejb.pk-field
 * @ejb.persistence
 * @ejb.interface-method
 */
```

```
public abstract Integer getId( );
public abstract void setId(Integer id);
```

Some additional support methods, such as the `ejbCreate` method on TaskBean, also need to change signatures:

```
/** @ejb.create-method */
public Intenger ejbCreate(String name)
    throws CreateException
{
    setName(name);
    return null;
}
```

The changes don't ripple far. We've provided an alternate version of the ToDo application in the *todo2* directory that contains the minimal changes to the session façade and to the JSF commands for this.

With that refactoring out of the way, let's see how to get JBoss to fill in the ID values. Key generation is accomplished by associating an entity command to an entity bean. The job of the entity command is to insert a newly created bean into the database while figuring out what the primary key should be.

In this example, you'll use a simple auto increment column in the database. In Hypersonic, whenever a row is inserted into a table with an identity column, Hypersonic will generate the next sequential key number and make it available to the client through a subsequent CALL IDENTITY( ) statement.

The entity command that understands how to generate sequential keys is `hsqldb-fetch-key`. To set this as the entity command for all entity beans, add an `entity-command` declaration to the `defaults` section of *jbosscmp-jdbc.xml*:

```
<defaults>
    <create-table>true</create-table>
    <alter-table>true</alter-table>
    <remove-table>true</remove-table>
    <entity-command name="hsqldb-fetch-key" />
</defaults>
```

Now, mark each primary key field as an `auto-increment` field:

```
<entity>
    <ejb-name>Task</ejb-name>
    <table-name>TODO_TASK</table-name>
    <cmp-field>
        <field-name>id</field-name>
        <column-name>TASK_ID</column-name>
        <auto-increment />
    </cmp-field>
    <!-- other CMP fields -->
</entity>
```

Notice that the ejbCreate method doesn't set the ID anymore. JBoss will fill in the value, just as it is doing for the user and started-Date fields, which are filled in from the audit data.

That's all there is to it. You can deploy the application from the *todo2* directory using the same build options as for the original application:

```
[todo2]$ ant main deploy
```

When you deploy the application, JBoss will create the new schema, marking the primary key as an identity column:

```
CREATE TABLE TODO_TASK
(
    TASK_ID INTEGER NOT NULL IDENTITY,
    TASK_NAME VARCHAR(256),
    TASK_USER VARCHAR(256),
    TASK_START TIMESTAMP,
    TASK_END TIMESTAMP,
    CONSTRAINT PK_TODO_TASK PRIMARY KEY (TASK_ID)
)
```

One advantage that numeric keys have over UUID keys is that simple numeric keys are much more readable. Looking over the TODO_TASK table is so much easier now.

Try creating a few tasks and watch the IDs in the TODO_TASK table increment with each newly created task.

What just happened?

You saw how to enable primary key generation in JBoss. All you had to do was to select the appropriate entity command and attach it to the application. You also could have associated the entity command with a specific bean, but generally you'll want key generation to work the same for all the entity beans in your application.

What about...

...other databases?

Each database supports different mechanisms for key generation. For MySQL, mysql-get-generated-keys makes use of the getGeneratedKeys function. The oracle-sequence entity command understands how to work with Oracle sequences. Check the *standardjbosscmp-jdbc.xml* file for the full set of database-specific entity commands.

...what about using your own key generator?

It is possible to write your own entity command, but that is no small task. Instead, you should look at the key-generator entity command. It interfaces with the JBoss key generator factory MBean, which you can easily replace with a factory that provides your own custom key generator.

Managing and Monitoring
JBoss

No matter how well you design and implement an application, some-thing always ends up going wrong. Your machine runs low on memory. The database stops accepting connections at 3:00 in the morning. Or maybe your application is running a bit more sluggish than normal. Things go wrong all the time. It's just a part of being a developer.

Fortunately, it is easy to get under the hood of JBoss and find out what is wrong. Because every service is loaded and managed by the JBoss microkernel, every service can be exposed and managed through the various JBoss management tools.

One interface to the service is the JMX Console. You've been using this simple web application throughout the book to inspect and manage JBoss services. Another web application is called the Web Console. It is a more advanced version of the JMX Console that provides basic monitor-ing and alerting functions. You'll learn how to use the Web Console in this chapter.

JBoss also provides a programmatic interface into management opera-tions. You'll see how to write code that can remotely inspect and man-age the server, and you'll learn how to use the twiddle application from the command line to access management features.

These capabilities might not seem quite as exciting as others we've talked about, but you'll appreciate having them when you are up late at night, working on a problem. So, let's dive in and see what's available.

Starting the Web Console

Since you've already been using the JMX Console, we'll skip right to its big brother, the Web Console. The Web Console is really just the standard JMX

The Web Console application is named console-mgr.sar, and you can find it in the deploy/management directory.

Console you've been using, with the addition of an applet that provides a higher-level view of the server. Instead of showing the raw managed beans (MBeans), the Web Console provides multiple views into the server, giving you the ability to more quickly find things that interest you.

How do I do that?

The Web Console is a simple web application that lives under the web-console context root. To start it up, open your browser and go to *http://localhost:8080/web-console/*. The page loads a Java applet, and it can take a few seconds to completely start up. Once it does, you should see something pretty close to what is in Figure 8-1.

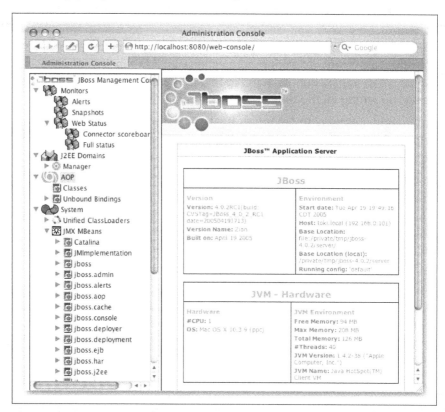

Figure 8-1. Web Console main page

There are two sections to the application. The lefthand side is the navigation panel. Clicking most items in the navigation panel will bring up a details page on the right. Clicking the JBoss logo will load the status page shown in Figure 8-1. If you right-click the logo, you'll have the option to refresh the navigation panel and sync up with the server. You'll also find that the shutdown command is accessible from that menu.

The navigation panel provides four basic views into the system:

Monitors

The Monitors section provides a quick link to the alerts and snapshots you've created. Those will be empty now, but you'll see items there later, when we look at how to create them.

J2EE Domains

The J2EE Domains section shows all the deployed applications and services, organized by the name of the deployment package.

AOP

The AOP section shows the status of the AOP-based applications currently deployed.

System

The System section shows all the MBeans in the system, organized by domain.

Take a minute to familiarize yourself with how the Web Console operates before moving on. We're going to be covering a lot of ground here.

AOP stands for aspect-oriented programming. AOP application deployment is one of the many non-J2EE services available in JBoss. For more information, see http:// aop.jboss.org/.

Monitoring Your Application

The most important thing in the server is your application, so we'll start our tour of JBoss's management and monitoring capabilities by looking at what JBoss can tell you about the state of currently running applications.

How do I do that?

If you drill down into the J2EE Domains section, you'll find an entry for the currently running JBoss instance. Inside that you'll find all the application packages deployed in the server: EAR files, WAR files, EJB jar files, and JBoss SAR (service archive) files. For deployments that are nested, such as with an EAR file, you can expand the parent archive to see the internal applications.

If the ToDo application is still deployed, you should find *todo.ear* near the top of the list. Selecting *todo.ear* will display some basic deployment information, including the *application.xml* deployment descriptor, in the details section on the right.

An EAR file is really just a container for other deployments, so there isn't much to see here. What you'll want to see are the contents of the EAR file. When you expand *todo.ear*, you'll see the two primary application components: *todo.jar* and *todo.war*.

Selecting either of these will show deployment information for the archive, just as you saw for the EAR file. Even better, expanding either of these archives will show all the EJBs or servlets provided by that application. Figure 8-2 shows the view of the TaskMaster bean.

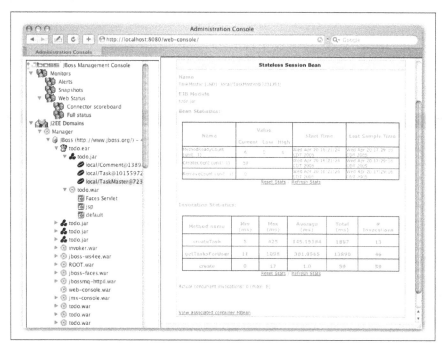

Figure 8-2. EJB statistics provided by the Web Console

The Bean Statistics section shows the status of the bean pool. JBoss currently has six instances of the TaskMaster bean waiting to serve requests. CreateCount shows the number of times a TaskMaster bean has been created, meaning an object was taken from the bean pool and made ready to service client requests.

Below that are the bean's invocation statistics. For each bean method, the total number of invocations processed is recorded, along with the minimum, maximum, and average processing time. You can see that, on average, it takes 145ms to create a new task, but 301ms to load all the tasks for a user. That load time seems a bit high, but it is actually skewed somewhat by the initial loading of data from the database. Once JBoss has cached the data, load times trend toward the minimum access time.

Chapter 8: Managing and Monitoring JBoss

You can verify this by resetting the statistics, using the Reset Stats link, and accessing the application again.

You can find similar processing statistics for a servlet by selecting a servlet under *todo.war*. The ToDo application doesn't use servlets extensively. The only interesting servlet is FacesServlet, which processes JavaServer Faces requests. If you select it, you will see the minimum, maximum, and average response times for the servlet, as well as an invocation count.

If you are a J2EE guru, you might recognize this as the JSR-77 J2EE Management data.

What just happened?

You saw how to get basic usage statistics out of the server, down to the bean and servlet level. The available information isn't exhaustive, but it will help you locate performance problems for further investigation.

Working with MBeans

MBeans are the management interfaces to the services registered with the JBoss microkernel. Every service in JBoss is represented by an MBean, and you have the ability to jump in and interact with those services.

You've been using the JMX Console throughout the book to access MBeans. You've looked at datasource statistics, checked which classloader loaded a specific class, and even shut down the server through the JMX Console, so you should be feeling comfortable with general MBean operation. In this lab we'll look at MBeans through the eyes of the Web Console, which adds a few new twists to what you've seen so far.

Only attributes whose type has a JavaBeans property editor defined can be edited through the Web Console. You can define new property editors using PropertyEditor-ManagerService.

How do I do that?

To get to the MBeans, expand the JMX MBeans node in the System section of the navigation panel. You should find the same MBeans you saw in the JMX Console, but the tree view presentation in the Web Console makes it a bit easier to navigate.

Let's find the jboss.system:type=ServerInfo MBean we used earlier in the book. Find the jboss.system domain and expand it. You should see the MBeans shown in Figure 8-3.

When you select jboss.system:type=ServerInfo, the MBean page from the JMX Console will show up in the details panel. There are two parts to the management interface displayed: attributes and operations.

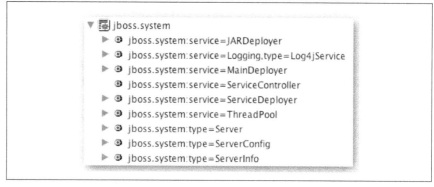

Figure 8-3. The MBeans in the jboss.system domain

Attributes typically represent the state or configuration of a service. Attributes are like fields on an object; they have a name, a type, and a value. They also have an access flag that specifies whether the attribute is readable or writable. Only writable attributes will show up as editable in the Web Console.

The `ServerInfo` MBean provides information about the state of the server, so all the attributes are read-only. Some of them are static, such as OS name and version. Others, such as the free memory and thread count values, will change regularly. You'll likely see those values change if you refresh the page.

You'll see a nicer way to monitor a changing value shortly.

To see an editable attribute, go back to the navigation panel and find the `jboss.system:service=Logging,type=log4j` MBean you used in Chapter 6. You can adjust the `RefreshPeriod` attribute to ask JBoss to check the *log4j.xml* file for changes more frequently. To change the value, enter the new value in the input box and click Apply Changes. After JBoss changes the configuration of the underlying service, the page will refresh and you will see the new value reflected on the MBean.

MBeans also provide management operations. These are just like methods on a regular Java object. Some operations are intended to send messages to the service. An example of this would be asking a connection pool to flush its pool, or changing the log levels in the log4j service.

If you are running Java 1.5, JBoss will provide a full stack trace for each thread too!

Other operations are purely informational. The ServerInfo MBean provides a `listThreadDump` operation that shows all the threads in the JVM. To invoke the operation, click the Invoke button next to the operation's name.

```
Total Threads: 42
Total Thread Groups: 7

Thread Group: system : max priority:10, demon:false
Thread: Reference Handler : priority:10, demon:true
```

```
Thread: Finalizer : priority:8, demon:true
Thread: Signal Dispatcher : priority:10, demon:true
Thread: CompileThread0 : priority:10, demon:true
Thread: RMI TCP Accept-1098 : priority:5, demon:true
Thread: RMI Reaper : priority:5, demon:false
Thread: GC Daemon : priority:2, demon:true
Thread: RMI TCP Accept-4444 : priority:5, demon:true

Thread Group: main : max priority:10, demon:false
Thread: DestroyJavaVM : priority:5, demon:false

Thread Group: jboss : max priority:10, demon:false
Thread: Thread-0 : priority:5, demon:true
Thread: ScannerThread : priority:5, demon:true
Thread: Thread-2 : priority:5, demon:true
Thread: PooledInvokerAcceptor#0-4445 : priority:5, demon:false
Thread: ContainerBackgroundProcessor[StandardEngine[jboss.web]] : priority:
5, demon:true
Thread: JBossMQ Cache Reference Softner : priority:5, demon:true
Thread: Thread-3 : priority:5, demon:true
Thread: HSQLDB Timer @4038e2 : priority:5, demon:true
Thread: Thread-5 : priority:5, demon:true
Thread: JCA PoolFiller : priority:5, demon:false
Thread: TimeoutFactory : priority:5, demon:true
Thread: Thread-6 : priority:5, demon:true
Thread: JBossLifeThread : priority:5, demon:false
Thread: http-0.0.0.0-8080 : priority:5, demon:true
Thread: http-0.0.0.0-8080-1 : priority:5, demon:true
Thread: TP-Processor1 : priority:5, demon:true
Thread: TP-Processor2 : priority:5, demon:true
Thread: TP-Processor3 : priority:5, demon:true
Thread: TP-Processor4 : priority:5, demon:true
Thread: TP-Monitor : priority:5, demon:true
Thread: http-0.0.0.0-8080-2 : priority:5, demon:true
Thread: http-0.0.0.0-8080-3 : priority:5, demon:true
Thread: http-0.0.0.0-8080-4 : priority:5, demon:true
Thread: http-0.0.0.0-8080-5 : priority:5, demon:true
Thread: http-0.0.0.0-8080-6 : priority:5, demon:true
Thread: http-0.0.0.0-8080-7 : priority:5, demon:true
Thread: http-0.0.0.0-8080-8 : priority:5, demon:true
Thread: http-0.0.0.0-8080-9 : priority:5, demon:true
Thread: http-0.0.0.0-8080-10 : priority:5, demon:true

Thread Group: JBoss Pooled Threads : max priority:10, demon:false
Thread: ClassLoadingPool(2)-1 : priority:5, demon:true
Thread: WorkManager(3)-1 : priority:5, demon:true

Thread Group: System Threads : max priority:10, demon:false
Thread: JBoss System Threads(1)-1 : priority:5, demon:true

Thread Group: JBossMQ Server Threads : max priority:10, demon:false
Thread: UILServerILService Accept Thread : priority:5, demon:false

Thread Group: RMI Runtime : max priority:10, demon:false
```

Another good informational bean is the JNDIView MBean. Find the `jboss:service=JNDIView` MBean and invoke the `list` operation. You'll get a complete dump of the JNDI tree for the server, including the enterprise naming contexts for your EJBs. Here's the part of the output for *todo.jar*:

```
Ejb Module: todo.jar

java:comp namespace of the Task bean:
+- env (class: org.jnp.interfaces.NamingContext)

java:comp namespace of the Comment bean:
+- env (class: org.jnp.interfaces.NamingContext)

java:comp namespace of the TaskMaster bean:
+- env (class: org.jnp.interfaces.NamingContext)
   |   +- ejb (class: org.jnp.interfaces.NamingContext)
   |   |   +- CommentLocal[link -> local/Comment@13898049]
   |   |       (class: javax.naming.LinkRef)
   |   |   +- TaskLocal[link -> local/Task@10155972]
   |   |       (class: javax.naming.LinkRef)
```

You can clearly see how the JNDI references were resolved. The JNDIView MBean is very useful when you are trying to find where an object is in the JNDI tree.

What just happened?

You saw how to interact with MBeans in the server through the Web Console. You can view and modify attributes and invoke management operations on any service in JBoss. There is very little you can't do through the MBean management interfaces.

Monitoring MBeans

What's the big deal with MBeans? Why are they interesting? MBeans provide a standardized form of metadata that management clients can use to inspect the state of the server. These self-describing services make it easy to write management applications, such as the Web Console, that can manage services regardless of their type.

In this environment, a management application can perform its actions on arbitrary services. It can monitor free memory in the system as easily as it can watch your connection pool size, and it can monitor services inside your application as easily as it monitors the JBoss-provided services.

With that in mind, we'll look at the ability to monitor a service, live, in JBoss.

How do I do that?

One of the things that can be valuable to watch in JBoss is the amount of free memory available to you. To do that, find the jboss.system: type=ServerInfo MBean in the navigation panel. Once you are there, expand the ServerInfo MBean so that you can see all the attributes. Right-click the FreeMemory attribute, and then bring up the context-sensitive menu, as shown in Figure 8-4.

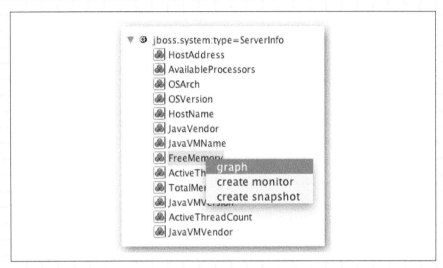

Figure 8-4. Free Memory graph menu

Choose the Graph menu item. JBoss will begin graphing the amount of free memory over time. If you leave it open for a while, you should see a graph that looks like Figure 8-5, showing free memory growing and shrinking as you go through the normal Java garbage-collection cycles.

You can right-click the graph to change its look, and even save or print the current view.

What just happened?

You saw how to get a live chart of the free memory in the JBoss application server. Although the charts themselves are somewhat limited, they are easy to set up. If you are trying to monitor a queue or connection pool size, it is easy to watch the response of the desired metric as you are accessing the application.

If you exposed parts of your application through MBeans, you can easily monitor application-specific values.

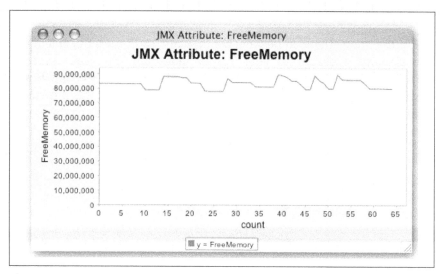

Figure 8-5. Free Memory graph

Creating a Snapshot

Live charts are powerful, but you aren't always sitting with the Web Console open, waiting for your application to run out of database connections. No, that always happens at 3:00 in the morning! Other problems manifest themselves slowly, over time.

JBoss gives you the ability to capture data over regular intervals. JBoss will collect observations of a specific MBean attribute. You can start or stop the data collection process according to your needs. Then you can return later to analyze the collected values.

Only numeric values can be graphed or monitored.

How do I do that?

To create a snapshot over time, choose the Create Snapshot menu item on the specific attribute you want to monitor. You'll be presented with a simple configuration form. You only need to enter the measurement time period. This is the time between measurements, in milliseconds. To monitor the value every two seconds, enter 2000 in the corresponding text field and click the Create button.

You can see the Manage Snapshot page in Figure 8-6.

To start the snapshot of memory usage, click the Start Snapshot button. Wait a few seconds for JBoss to collect measurements, and then click the Graph Dataset button. That will give you a graph like the one shown in Figure 8-7.

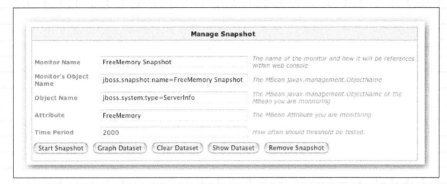

Figure 8-6. Manage snapshot

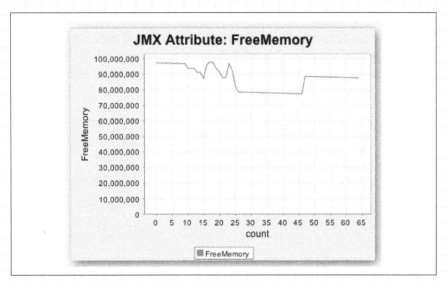

Figure 8-7. Snapshot graph

Notice that the graph isn't a live graph. It's a fixed graph of the data collected up to that point. This graph will give you a good idea of what happened over the specified time period. If you need better analysis capabilities, click Show Dataset, which displays all the collected data. You can select the data in the dataset view, and copy and paste it to an application such as Excel that can perform more sophisticated numerical analysis.

Creating a Monitor

A snapshot is good for collecting information about one aspect of your server over time, to gain an understanding of your server's behavior, and to find anomalies. However, when you are looking for a specific problem, you generally want to know about it as soon as that problem has occurred. Then you can go to a long-running snapshot and examine how the server behaved during the time leading up to the problem.

The Web Console gives you the ability to create an alert to monitor an MBean attribute value for a specific condition. When that condition is met, JBoss triggers a notification event to alert you to the condition. In this lab, you will create a monitor on the free memory of the JBoss application server.

How do I do that?

To create the alert, find the FreeMemory attribute of the jboss.system: type=ServerInfo MBean one more time and choose Create Monitor from the menu. The details section of the Web Console will contain the monitor creation form shown in Figure 8-8.

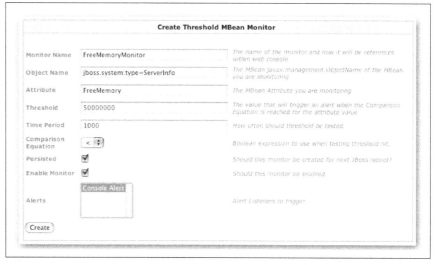

Figure 8-8. Creating an alert

JBoss has filled in the MBean name and attribute name. The Threshold and Comparison Equation values determine the trigger for the event. Monitors are purely numeric and can be compared to any fixed value. This monitor will trigger an alert when free memory goes below 50,000,00, which is approximately 50MB. JBoss checks the monitor every Time Period milliseconds.

If the alert is triggered, JBoss will send an alert to the alert handlers selected in the Alerts select box. Right now only one alert handler is listed: `Console Alert`. It sends an alert message to the console log. You'll see some other alert options later.

Select the `Persist Changes` and `Enable Monitor` boxes to make sure the alert will be persisted and enabled before clicking the Create button.

You've created a monitor to generate an alert when free memory falls below a certain threshold, but where did the monitor go? All the monitors are listed in the Alerts section of the navigation pane. However, you may need to refresh the tree to see the Alerts section.

Right-click the JBoss logo to refresh the tree.

When you select the Alerts node, you'll see a list of all active monitors. The list looks like that shown in Figure 8-9.

Monitors and Monitor Status

Status	Monitor Name	Observed MBean	Observed Attribute	
OK	FreeMemoryMonitor	jboss.system:type=ServerInfo	FreeMemory	manage

Figure 8-9. The list of active monitors

The green OK status means the monitor has not yet triggered an alert.

To prove that our alert works, we need to force JBoss to trigger it. To do that, we need a way to consume lots of memory, driving the free memory below the 50MB threshold. We've created a simple JSP to do that:

```jsp
<%@ page import="java.util.*" %>

<h1> Memory Eater </h1>
<%! int count; %>
<%
    try {
        ArrayList list = new ArrayList( );
        while (true) {
            list.add(new Object( ));
            count++;
        }

    } catch (Throwable t) {
    }

%>

Created <%= count %> objects...
```

This JSP continually creates objects until memory runs so low that an exception is thrown. Copy this JSP directly into *ROOT.war* in the *deploy/ jbossweb-tomcat55.sar* directory to make it available.

If you name the file *memory.jsp*, you can access it at *http://localhost: 8080/memory.jsp*. When you access it, the server will spin for a while as it eats up memory. Unless you have a large amount of memory and a slow CPU, it shouldn't take more than about 15 seconds to deplete the free memory in the JVM. When the page finally loads, you should see that the alert shows up in your console log as expected:

```
14:16:39,171 INFO  [ConsoleAlertListener] FreeMemoryMonitor was triggered
for attribute FreeMemory.
```

If you return to the list of monitors, you will see that the status has changed from a green OK to a red ALERT. If you click Manage, you'll see the monitor with the Triggered Value filled in. This is the value at the time the threshold was exceeded. Figure 8-10 shows the value in this case.

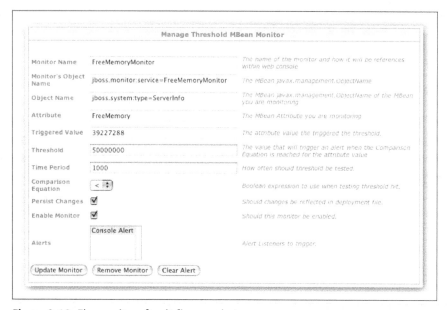

Figure 8-10. The monitor after it fires an alert

As you can see, the value was well below 50MB by the time JBoss noticed. The JSP was consuming memory very rapidly, and even though the monitor was very aggressive in checking the value every second, it didn't notice until the measure was well below the threshold.

Normally, the values you are monitoring won't change so rapidly, but you do need to be careful to pick a time period for the monitor that is likely to pick up the change. If we monitored free memory every minute, the event may have come and gone by the time JBoss checked the value again, and you would have missed the event.

Chapter 8: Managing and Monitoring JBoss

What just happened?

You created a monitor and triggered an alert using the Web Console. There's not much more to say, but we should point out that once a monitor has issued an alert, it remains in that state until you clear it. The Clear Alert button clears the alert and restarts the monitor.

Creating an Email Alert

When you created the monitor, you chose to send the alert to the console alert listener, and JBoss logged the alert as an INFO message waiting to be read. Alert listeners don't need to be so passive. In this lab, you'll configure alerts to be sent by email.

If you need an email server for testing, you can try the JBoss Mail Server.

How do I do that?

You send email alerts using the email service, so first you'll need to make sure the email service is properly configured. Look in the *mail-service. xml* file. If you have a local mail server that relays without authentication, you can put the hostname of the server in the mail.smtp.host property and be done with the mail service.

If you do need to authenticate to the mail server, you will need to set the User and Password attributes with the required login, and set mail.smtp. auth to true:

```
<mbean code="org.jboss.mail.MailService"
      name="jboss:service=Mail">
    <attribute name="JNDIName">java:/Mail</attribute>
    <attribute name="User">username</attribute>
    <attribute name="Password">my password</attribute>
    <attribute name="Configuration">
        <configuration>
            <!-- … -->
            <property name="mail.smtp.host"
                      value="my.mail.server"/>
            <property name="mail.smtp.auth"
                      value="true" />
        </configuration>
    </attribute>
</mbean>
```

Any standard JavaMail configuration options can be placed here. If your mail server is particularly demanding, you might need to consult the JavaMail documentation at *http://java.sun.com/products/javamail/* to find the correct properties. Here's an example of a JavaMail configuration to connect to GMail:

```
<property name="mail.smtp.host"                    value="smtp.gmail.com"/>
<property name="mail.smtp.port"                    value="465"/>
<property name="mail.smtp.auth"                    value="true" />
<property name="mail.smtp.starttls.enable"         value="true" />
<property name="mail.smtp.socketFactory.port"      value="465" />
<property name="mail.smtp.socketFactory.fallback" value="false" />
<property name="mail.smtp.socketFactory.class"
          value="javax.net.ssl.SSLSocketFactory" />
```

That gets the mail service running. You can configure the email alert listener by uncommenting the `EmailAlertListener` MBean in *monitoring-service.xml*. You'll need to set the To and From addresses for the email message as shown here:

```
<mbean code="org.jboss.monitor.alerts.EmailAlertListener"
       name="jboss.alerts:service=EmailAlertListener">
    <depends>jboss:service=Mail</depends>
    <attribute name="MessageTemplate"><![CDATA[
        %(MONITOR_NAME) was triggered for attribute %(ATTRIBUTE).
    ]]></attribute>
    <attribute name="AlertName">Email Alert</attribute>
    <attribute name="To">jbossnotebook@gmail.com</attribute>
    <attribute name="From">jbossnotebook@gmail.com</attribute>
    <attribute name="ReplyTo">jbossnotebook@gmail.com</attribute>
    <attribute name="SubjectTemplate">
        <![CDATA[[jboss-alert] %(MONITOR_NAME)]]>
    </attribute>
</mbean>
```

Once you have made these changes, the free memory monitor will show an Email Alert option in the Alerts box. After you add the email listener to the monitor, you should access *memory.jsp* again to trigger the alert. If your email service is configured properly, you should soon have an email alert in your inbox. Figure 8-11 shows an email alert viewed from within GMail.

It's not the most informative of messages, but it works. You can change the message title and body by changing the `MessageTemplate` and `SubjectTemplate` attributes on the `EmailAlertListener` MBean.

Figure 8-11. An email alert viewed in GMail

What just happened?

You configured a monitor to send an alert message by email. To do that you had to first enable the mail service to know what mail server to use to send mail. Then you activated the email alert listener service. The Web Console immediately saw the email alert listener and let you connect your monitor to it.

If email isn't good enough, you can write your own listener to process alerts.

Managing JBoss from the Command Line

The Web Console gives you access to all the services in JBoss, but it does have one huge limitation. It is a web application that requires that an interactive user do the pointing and clicking. That's fine most of the time, but sometimes you'll want to automate access to the server.

JBoss provides a very simple command-line application, called twiddle, that lets you query MBeans, get and set attribute values, and even invoke operations. If you need to automate access to JBoss, twiddle is the easiest and best tool to use.

How do I do that?

The twiddle script sits in the *bin* directory, next to the startup and shutdown scripts. You can run it from any terminal window, and it's easy to use. The get command lets you query an MBean by name. Pass in the name of the MBean and a list of attributes to retrieve:

```
[bin]$ ./twiddle.sh get jboss.system:type=ServerInfo FreeMemory ActiveThreadCount
FreeMemory=90167064
ActiveThreadCount=46
```

If you don't specify any attributes, you'll get all of them:

```
[bin]$ ./twiddle.sh get jboss.system:type=ServerInfo
HostAddress=192.168.0.101
AvailableProcessors=1
OSArch=ppc
OSVersion=10.3.9
HostName=toki.local
JavaVendor=Apple Computer, Inc.
JavaVMName=Java HotSpot(TM) Client VM
FreeMemory=90898472
ActiveThreadGroupCount=6
TotalMemory=132775936
JavaVMVersion=1.4.2-38
ActiveThreadCount=45
JavaVMVendor="Apple Computer, Inc."
```

```
OSName=Mac OS X
JavaVersion=1.4.2_05
MaxMemory=218103808
```

If you need to use a value in a script, use the --noprefix flag:

```
[bin]$ ./twiddle.sh get --noprefix jboss.system:type=ServerInfo FreeMemory
92063536
```

The set command sets an attribute value on an MBean. This command sets the connection pool size for DefaultDS to 25:

```
[bin]$ ./twiddle.sh set jboss.jca:name=DefaultDS,service=ManagedConnectionPool \
MaxSize 25
MaxSize=25
```

You can invoke MBean operations using the invoke command. The output will be the return value, if any, of the method. This command asks for garbage collection to be run:

```
[bin]$ ./twiddle.sh invoke jboss.system:type=Server runGarbageCollector
```

If you check the console log, you will see the results of running garbage collection:

```
18:28:57,779 INFO  [Server] Total/free memory: 132775936/91869984
18:28:59,429 INFO  [Server] Hinted to the JVM to run garbage collection
18:28:59,431 INFO  [Server] Total/free memory: 132775936/92366288
```

The following example invokes the clearAlert method on the free memory monitor:

```
[bin]$ ./twiddle.sh invoke jboss.monitor:service=FreeMemoryMonitor \
clearAlert
```

If you are on a remote machine, add the -s option to specify the host you are trying to talk to:

```
[bin]$ ./twiddle.sh -s hostname invoke jboss.system:type=Server shutdown
```

You can run that command from any remote machine to shut down your JBoss instance.

What just happened?

You accessed the MBeans on your JBoss instance from a remote machine using the twiddle command-line script. twiddle gives you fast, scriptable access to any JBoss instance.

CHAPTER 9

Rolling Out JBoss

JBoss comes in a state that is extremely developer friendly. JBoss doesn't use an installer and doesn't require any additional configuration to start. In most cases, your application won't require any JBoss-specific configuration to deploy and run. The default configuration comes with the services most commonly needed, already running and in a state that makes them easily accessible.

It is an ideal world for developers, but when the time comes to put your application in production, you really won't want your application server to be so friendly. You'll want to limit the services provided to just the ones you need, especially when those services offer entry points for the outside world to access the server, and you'll want to make sure the remaining services are configured in a production-friendly manner. In this chapter, we'll walk through the default JBoss installation and see what updates are needed to get a JBoss instance ready to be exposed to the outside world.

As we go through the services, keep in mind that although they require a bit of work, you'll need to do this work only once. You learned how to create a new server configuration in Chapter 1. We recommend that you create a server configuration for your deployment environment. You can use this configuration as the starting point for any installation you do, and you'll be sure that each machine has identically configured services.

Securing the Management Consoles

You've used the JMX Console and Web Console applications extensively throughout the book. Given that you can completely control a JBoss

In this chapter:
- *Securing the Management Consoles*
- *Securing the JMX Invoker*
- *Removing the HTTP Invokers*
- *Configuring the JMS Invokers*
- *Removing Hypersonic*
- *Configuring Tomcat Connectors*
- *Setting a Root Web Application*
- *Removing the Class Download Service*

For consistency, we'll continue to work from the default configuration in these examples.

instance through those applications, you might have found it a bit odd that you never had to specify a username and password to access them.

Both applications are accessible to anyone who has access to your server. If you plan to use those applications, you'll need to perform a few configuration steps to get them ready.

How do I do that?

Before we start, it should be obvious that if you don't need the management consoles, you can get rid of them and not need to worry about whether remote users can access them. The JMX Console lives in *deploy/jmx-console.war* and the Web Console lives in *deploy/management*. If you remove both of those directories, JBoss will forget all about the management applications.

Unfortunately, by removing those directories you also lose the ability to manage your server through them. In some cases this makes perfect sense, but we think the management consoles are useful enough that you'll want to keep them around.

If you decide you want to keep them around, you'll need to link them to a security domain and apply security to the web applications, just as you did for the ToDo application. To make things easier, JBoss provides pre-configured, but commented out, security declarations that you just need to enable.

In the *jmx-console.war* directory, you'll need to edit *WEB-INF/web.xml* by uncommenting the following security constraint:

```
<security-constraint>
    <web-resource-collection>
        <web-resource-name>HtmlAdaptor</web-resource-name>
        <description>
            An example security config that only allows users with the
            role JBossAdmin to access the HTML JMX console web application
        </description>
        <url-pattern>/*</url-pattern>
        <http-method>GET</http-method>
        <http-method>POST</http-method>
    </web-resource-collection>
    <auth-constraint>
        <role-name>JBossAdmin</role-name>
    </auth-constraint>
</security-constraint>
```

This restricts the entire JMX Console to users with the JBossAdmin role. If you recall the security discussion in Chapter 5, you'll remember that along with this you'll need to link to the security domain in *WEB-INF/ jboss-web.xml*:

```
<jboss-web>
    <security-domain>java:/jaas/jmx-console</security-domain>
</jboss-web>
```

This security domain is already deployed:

```
<application-policy name="jmx-console">
    <authentication>
        <login-module
            code="org.jboss.security.auth.spi.UsersRolesLoginModule"
            flag="required">
            <module-option name="usersProperties">
                props/jmx-console-users.properties
            </module-option>
            <module-option name="rolesProperties">
                props/jmx-console-roles.properties
            </module-option>
        </login-module>
    </authentication>
</application-policy>
```

You saw in Chapter 5 how to replace and customize a security domain. For now, we'll stick with the properties file mechanism. The two properties files mentioned, *jmx-console-users.properties* and *jmx-console-roles. properties*, are in the *conf/props* directory. Keeping the files in a shared location rather than in the web application directory allows you to later share the user information with the Web Console.

The two properties files declare a user named admin whose password is admin. You might want to take the time to change that now. Keeping the default name and password for the JMX Console is nearly as bad as not protecting it at all.

That's all you have to do for the JMX Console. Now we'll make the same changes to the Web Console. You'll have to look all the way down in *management/console-mgr.sar/web-console.war/WEB-INF* to find the configuration files for the Web Console.

You'll need to uncomment the security constraint in *web.xml*, and set a security domain in *jboss-web.xml*. Instead of uncommenting the java:/ jaas/web-console security domain currently referenced, set the security domain to java:/jass/jmx-console. This will cause both applications to be authenticated from the same security domain, instead of using two separate logins for the applications.

Although you can redeploy the applications, the fastest way to make the changes take hold is to restart the server.

What just happened?

You added user security to the two management console applications. When you access either of them, JBoss will ask you to log in. The *jmx-console-users.properties* and *jmx-console-roles.properties* files in the *conf/props* directory provide the authentication information, but you can change the authentication details in *login-config.xml*.

There is still one problem here. If you access the management consoles over normal HTTP, your username and password are sent in the clear. You should enable SSL, as shown in Chapter 5, and always access the application over HTTPS when connecting over a nontrusted network.

Securing the JMX Invoker

The management consoles are not the only management access points into the system. The shutdown and twiddle scripts are programs that interact with JBoss at a management level. They don't use the web applications. Instead, they interact with the JMX invoker.

An invoker is a service in JBoss that accepts *invocations*, which are requests for actions to be performed on the server, from external clients. To interact with the JMX microkernel, you use the JMX invoker.

Whenever you hear the term *invoker*, you should immediately wonder whether you really need to accept a particular kind of request from the outside world. If you don't, it is usually best to simply remove the invoker. You can remove the JMX invoker if you will never need to perform a remote shutdown or any sort of programmatic remote management. However, since those management actions are quite useful, we think it is better to leave the JMX invoker active and apply security to it.

How do I do that?

The JMX invoker service is configured in *deploy/jmx-invoker-service.xml* and is quite simple to secure. The invoke operation on the `jboss.jmx:type=adaptor,name=Invoker` managed bean (MBean) needs to have an authentication interceptor added to it that links to the appropriate security domain. That doesn't sound easy, but the appropriate interceptor is already in the file, waiting to be uncommented:

```
<descriptors>
    <interceptors>
        <interceptor
            code="org.jboss.jmx.connector.invoker.AuthenticationInterceptor"
            securityDomain="java:/jaas/jmx-console"/>
```

```
    </interceptors>
  </descriptors>
```

This requires the user to be authenticated by the java:/jaas/jmx-console security domain to invoke management operations remotely. To be sure the interceptor is working, try to shut down the server using the shutdown command:

```
[bin]$ ./shutdown.sh -S
Exception in thread "main" java.lang.SecurityException: Failed to
authenticate principal=null, securityDomain=jmx-console
        at org.jboss.jmx.connector.invoker.AuthenticationInterceptor.invoke(
            AuthenticationInterceptor.java:76)
        at org.jboss.mx.server.Invocation.invoke(Invocation.java:74)
        at ...
```

The shutdown script will fail unless you specify a valid username and password to the script. The -u and -p arguments specify the username and password, respectively:

```
[bin]$ sh ./shutdown.sh -S -u admin -p admin
```

If you have already removed the admin user or changed the password, make sure you use the correct username and password.

What just happened?

You secured the JMX invoker from unauthenticated access by attaching an authentication interceptor to it. This interceptor was linked to the java:/jaas/jmx-console security domain, allowing you to use the same administrative usernames and passwords you already defined for the JMX Console and Web Console applications.

Removing the HTTP Invokers

Invokers can be scary to have around because they give the outside world a potential access point to your server. When properly secured, they don't cause you much worry, but you do have to know they are there before you can make sure they are secure.

Invokers that listen on a specific port for remote connections are easy to track down. Standard networking tools such as nmap, lsof, and netstat can tell you what ports are in use on a machine. What isn't so easy is tracking down invokers that tunnel over other protocols, HTTP being the primary offender.

HTTP invocations are important. Oftentimes overzealous network administrators limit the access between two networks to port 80. That forces you, the developer, to find ways to tunnel application access over that one port. JBoss can perform every type of remote access over port 80: JNDI, JMX invocations, EJB invocations, etc....

JBoss is configured to allow access over HTTP by default; however, most applications don't need to tunnel over port 80. In that case, having the HTTP invokers is more of a liability, and the best policy is to just remove them.

How do I do that?

There's that pesky invoker word again.

Removing the HTTP invokers is easy. The HTTP invokers are managed by a single service, *http-invoker.sar*. Just remove that entire directory from the deploy directory and you will be all set, knowing that remote clients cannot access through the HTTP invoker back door.

Configuring the JMS Invokers

We didn't use messaging in the ToDo application, but messaging is an important part of many enterprise applications. JBoss supports JMS, the Java Message Service, and provides a fully spec-compliant JMS implementation, complete with invokers for accessing JMS destinations outside of the application server.

Fortunately, setting up JMS for production use is quite easy. You need to know only two things: whether your applications uses JMS, and whether external applications use your JMS. With those two pieces of information, you can configure the JMS invokers.

How do I do that?

All of the JMS services are configured under the *deploy/jms* directory. If you aren't using JMS at all, all you need to do is delete the entire *jms* directory. That will remove not only the JMS invokers, but also the entire JMS subsystem. If you aren't writing a messaging application, there's no need to take up valuable memory and processor time tending to those services.

JMS is common enough that we can't just leave it at that. If you do need to keep messaging around, you'll need to decide which JMS invokers to keep around.

The JMS invokers are the services in the *jms* directory. The first is *jvm-il-service.xml*. This invocation layer is used only inside the application servers. It doesn't provide any access to the outside world, so don't worry about leaving it around.

Next is *jbossmq-httpil.sar*. This is the HTTP invoker for JMS. If you need external clients that tunnel over HTTP, this invoker will save your life. But you likely won't need it, so just remove this service and don't worry about it.

The last invoker is *uil2-service.xml*. If you are curious, that stands for unified invocation layer, version 2. This gives access to JBoss messaging queues. If you have no external clients accessing your destinations, you can safely remove the service. Otherwise, you'll have to leave it and make sure your destinations are properly secured.

Destinations are configured in *jbossmq-destinations.xml* in *deploy/jms*. Here's the configuration for a topic:

```
<mbean code="org.jboss.mq.server.jmx.Topic"
       name="jboss.mq.destination:service=Topic,name=testTopic">
    <depends optional-attribute-name="DestinationManager">
        jboss.mq:service=DestinationManager
    </depends>
    <depends optional-attribute-name="SecurityManager">
        jboss.mq:service=SecurityManager
    </depends>
    <attribute name="SecurityConf">
        <security>
            <role name="guest"       read="true" write="true"/>
            <role name="publisher"   read="true" write="true"
                                     create="false"/>
            <role name="durpublisher" read="true" write="true"
                                     create="true"/>
        </security>
    </attribute>
</mbean>
```

The SecurityConf attribute defines the permissions for each logical role you are interested in. The read and write permissions correspond to the ability to read messages from and send messages to a destination. The create permission is the ability to create a durable subscription to a destination.

The SecurityManager attribute links to the security interceptor defined in jbossmq-service:

```
<mbean code="org.jboss.mq.security.SecurityManager"
       name="jboss.mq:service=SecurityManager">
    <attribute name="DefaultSecurityConfig">
        <security>
            <role name="guest" read="true" write="true" create="true"/>
        </security>
    </attribute>
```

```
<attribute name="SecurityDomain">java:/jaas/jbossmq</attribute>
<depends optional-attribute-name="NextInterceptor">
    jboss.mq:service=DestinationManager
</depends>
</mbean>
```

The security manager defines both the default security configuration, if one isn't defined on the destination in *jbossmq-destinations.xml*, and the security domain to be used to verify JMS permissions. `java:/jaas/jbossmq` is already defined in *login–config.xml*:

```
<application-policy name="jbossmq">
    <authentication>
        <login-module
            code="org.jboss.security.auth.spi.DatabaseServerLoginModule"
            flag="required">
            <module-option name="unauthenticatedIdentity">
                guest
            </module-option>
            <module-option name="dsJndiName">java:/DefaultDS</module-option>
            <module-option name="principalsQuery">
                SELECT PASSWD FROM JMS_USERS WHERE USERID=?
            </module-option>
            <module-option name="rolesQuery">
                SELECT ROLEID, 'Roles' FROM JMS_ROLES WHERE USERID=?
            </module-option>
        </login-module>
    </authentication>
</application-policy>
```

This is a standard `DatabaseServerLoginModule`. You saw how to configure it in Chapter 5. What's interesting about this configuration is the use of the `unauthenticatedIdentity` option. This says to assign unauthenticated users the guest role. When it's combined with the `DefaultSecurityConf` of the JMS security manager, anyone can access your JMS destinations. You'll want to remove the permissions for the guest role if you have remote access into JMS.

What just happened?

You saw the necessary steps to configure JMS in a production system. If you weren't using a service, you removed it completely. Otherwise, you had to choose which of the three invokers you needed. To allow remote JMS clients, you had to keep the UIL2 service, which required you to pay careful attention to the security configuration.

Removing Hypersonic

Hypersonic is a great database for testing an application, but it isn't production ready. In Chapter 4, you saw how to switch to another database. If you aren't using Hypersonic, you can remove the entire service. Hypersonic doesn't listen for connections from the outside world unless you ask it to, so you don't need to worry about securing it. However, you might not want an extra relational database hanging around in memory. It's fairly lightweight, but you'll probably be better off just getting rid of it.

How do I do that?

The *hsqldb-ds.xml* file not only configures the Hypersonic datasources, but also it has the MBeans that control the entire embedded database service. Removing this file will remove all traces of Hypersonic.

It sounds trivial, and it would be except that several other services depend on Hypersonic. We'll go through the changes now, assuming you have created a MySQL database as shown in Chapter 4, and that the ToDo application is already switched over to using that.

The first service is the EJB timer service, in ejb-deployer.xml. You should replace the reference to DefaultDS with a reference to the correct datasource. In Chapter 4, we chose the name MySqlDS. The change is simple:

```
<!-- A persistence policy that persists timers to a database -->
<mbean code="org.jboss.ejb.txtimer.DatabasePersistencePolicy"
     name="jboss.ejb:service=EJBTimerService,persistencePolicy=database">
    <!-- DataSource JNDI name -->
    <depends optional-attribute-name="DataSource">
        jboss.jca:service=DataSourceBinding,name=MySqlDS
    </depends>
    <!-- The plugin that handles database persistence -->
    <attribute name="DatabasePersistencePlugin">
        org.jboss.ejb.txtimer.GeneralPurposeDatabasePersistencePlugin
    </attribute>
</mbean>
```

JMS also requires persistence changes to be made. If you aren't using JMS and you chose to remove it from your configuration, you can stop here. Otherwise, go to the *deploy/jms* directory and look for *hsqldb-jdbc2-service.xml* and *hsqldb-jdbc-state-service.xml*.

hsqldb-jdbc2-service.xml controls message persistence. You can remove it completely and replace it with a database-specific file from *docs/examples/jms*. For MySQL, copy *mysql-jdbc2-service.xml* into the *jms* directory.

hsqldb-jdbc-state-service.xml isn't quite so simple. There are no database-specific templates for this. You'll need to update the datasource dependency manually:

```
<mbean code="org.jboss.mq.sm.jdbc.JDBCStateManager"
       name="jboss.mq:service=StateManager">
    <depends optional-attribute-name="ConnectionManager">
        jboss.jca:service=DataSourceBinding,name=MySqlDS
    </depends>
    <!-- ... -->
</mbean>
```

This datasource reference needs to be the same as the datasource you saw earlier, in the jbossmq security domain in *login-config.xml*. You'll want to update that now too:

```
<application-policy name="jbossmq">
    <authentication>
        <login-module
           code="org.jboss.security.auth.spi.DatabaseServerLoginModule"
           flag="required">
         <module-option name="unauthenticatedIdentity">guest
         </module-option>
         <module-option name="dsJndiName">java:/MySqlDS</module-option>
         <module-option name="principalsQuery">
             SELECT PASSWD FROM JMS_USERS WHERE USERID=?
         </module-option>
         <module-option name="rolesQuery">
             SELECT ROLEID, 'Roles' FROM JMS_ROLES WHERE USERID=?
         </module-option>
        </login-module>
    </authentication>
</application-policy>
```

The final dependency on DefaultDS is *uuid-key-generator.sar*. If you aren't using the JBoss UUID key generator, remove this service from the deploy directory. If you are, you'll need to update the *META-INF/jboss-service.xml* file to reference the preferred datasource:

```
<mbean code="org.jboss.ejb.plugins.keygenerator.hilo.
HiLoKeyGeneratorFactory"
         name="jboss:service=KeyGeneratorFactory,type=HiLo">
    <!-- ... -->
    <depends optional-attribute-name="DataSource">
        jboss.jca:service=DataSourceBinding,name=MySqlDS
    </depends>
    <!-- ... -->
</mbean>
```

Unfortunately, this service is not provided in exploded form, so you'll have you unpack the archive to get to it.

What just happened?

You removed Hypersonic and updated, or removed, the services that depend on it. All of the persistent services will write their tables into the new database. If you've kept them around and restarted JBoss, you should find several new database tables in your external database:

```
mysql> show tables in jbossdb;
+--------------------+
| Tables_in_jbossdb  |
+--------------------+
| Comment            |
| HILOSEQUENCES      |
| JMS_ROLES          |
| JMS_SUBSCRIPTIONS  |
| JMS_TRANSACTIONS   |
| JMS_USERS          |
| TIMERS             |
| Task               |
| jms_messages       |
+--------------------+
9 rows in set (0.14 sec)
```

You could have saved yourself some trouble by creating a replacement DefaultDS. Then it wouldn't have been necessary to change all the data-source references. However, it's important to be explicit about your configuration in a production machine. The extra effort is worth the peace of mind of knowing that all your persistent services are configured correctly.

Configuring Tomcat Connectors

In Tomcat, connectors allow web requests to come in from the outside world. Conceptually, they are like the invokers you saw earlier in this chapter, only they accept HTTP requests against web applications and not general invocation requests against services in JBoss. HTTP connectors aren't so innocuous when there are web applications such as the HTTP invoker, which translates HTTP requests into service invocations. However, you don't need to be concerned about HTTP connectors. The actual web applications behind them are the concern. Your only concern with connectors is to have the correct ones enabled and to have them listening on the right ports.

How do I do that?

Two connectors are defined in *jbossweb-tomcat55.sar/server.xml*. The first is the AJP connector that listens for requests proxied from an Apache server running mod_jk:

```
<!-- A AJP 1.3 Connector on port 8009 -->
<Connector port="8009" address="${jboss.bind.address}"
           emptySessionPath="true" enableLookups="false"
           redirectPort="8443" protocol="AJP/1.3"/>
```

This connector listens on port 8009, but since external clients do not see this port, it doesn't need to be changed. If you aren't using mod_jk, you can remove this connector to save resources.

The normal Tomcat service listens for HTTP requests on port 8080. The connector looks like this:

```
<Connector port="8080" address="${jboss.bind.address}"
           maxThreads="250" strategy="ms" maxHttpHeaderSize="8192"
           emptySessionPath="true"
           enableLookups="false" redirectPort="8443" acceptCount="100"
           connectionTimeout="20000" disableUploadTimeout="true"/>
```

If you have a Unix box and you change the port to something below 1024, you'll need to be running JBoss as root.

If your web server is directly visible to the outside world, you'll want to use the standard port 80, unless you have a frontend load balancer that can redirect the standard port 80 to 8080 on your machine. To do that, change the port attribute to 80.

There is a third connector you might add, the SSL connector. Chapter 5 showed you how to enable SSL, but you used port 8443 at the time. The standard HTTPS port is 443, so you'll want to change the port number on that connector. That SSL connector looks like this:

```
<Connector port="443" address="${jboss.bind.address}"
           maxThreads="100" strategy="ms" maxHttpHeaderSize="8192"
           emptySessionPath="true" scheme="https"
           secure="true" clientAuth="false"
           keystoreFile="${jboss.server.home.dir}/conf/ssl.keystore"
           keystorePass="mypassword" keyAlias="testkey1"
           sslProtocol="TLS" />
```

If you do use a different SSL port, you will need to make sure you change the redirect port of the HTTP connector port to be the SSL port (443). Both the HTTP and AJP connectors have a redirectPort attribute that should be set to the right value:

```
<Connector port="80" address="${jboss.bind.address}"
           maxThreads="250" strategy="ms" maxHttpHeaderSize="8192"
           emptySessionPath="true"
           enableLookups="false" redirectPort="443" acceptCount="100"
           connectionTimeout="20000" disableUploadTimeout="true"/>
```

Restart JBoss to make these changes take effect. You should be able to access the server at *http://localhost/* with no port number listed in the URL.

What just happened?

You saw where the Tomcat connectors are configured, and you changed the ports Tomcat uses for HTTP requests. There weren't any direct security concerns around the connectors. All you needed to worry about was making the right connectors available on the right ports.

What about...

...not being able to access the server on port 80?

Check the console log for errors as you start up. You may have another web server running on port 80 on your machine, or you may not be running as a user with permissions to access a privileged port such as port 80. The log messages will help you determine what is stopping JBoss from using port 80.

Setting a Root Web Application

When you access JBoss for the first time, JBoss provides you with the default root application, shown in Figure 9-1.

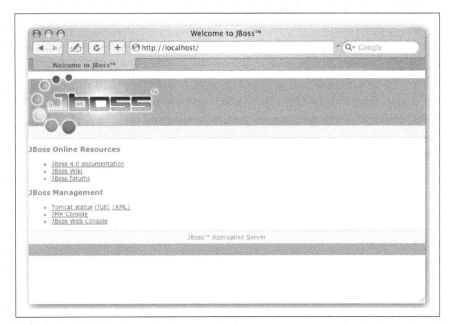

Figure 9-1. Default root application

In production, you'll want your own application to serve the root context.

How do I do that?

If you didn't change the HTTP port to 80, make sure you use http://localhost:8080/.

Controlling the context of a web application is different for WAR files deployed inside of an EAR file and for WAR files deployed as standalone files.

EAR files contain a standard J2EE mechanim for controlling the context of the web application. The `context-root` element of a web module in *application.xml* controls the root web application. Setting the root context to / will place the ToDo application at the root context. In the ToDo application the change will look like this:

```
<application xmlns="http://java.sun.com/xml/ns/j2ee" version="1.4"
    xmlns:xsi="http://www.w3.org/2001/XMLSchema-instance"
    xsi:schemaLocation="http://java.sun.com /xml/ns/j2ee
        http://java.sun.com/xml/ns/j2ee/application_1_4.xsd">
    <display-name>JBoss Notebook ToDo Application</display-name>
    <description>JBoss Notebook ToDo Application</description>
    <module>
        <ejb>todo.jar</ejb>
    </module>
    <module>
        <web>
            <web-uri>todo.war</web-uri>
            <context-root>/</context-root>
        </web>
    </module>
</application>
```

If you make this change and redeploy the application, accessing *http://localhost/* will bring you directly to the ToDo application.

JBoss won't complain if you have multiple applications wanting to serve the root context, but only the most recently deployed one will be active.

For a standalone WAR file, the context-root element should be added to *jboss-web.xml*. We'll go back to the quote machine web application from Chapter 2. Create a *jboss-web.xml* file in quote/src/metadata that looks like this:

```
<!DOCTYPE jboss-web PUBLIC
        "-//JBoss//DTD Web Application 2.4//EN"
        "http://www.jboss.org/j2ee/dtd/jboss-web_4_0.dtd">
<jboss-web>
        <context-root>/</context-root>
</jboss-web>.
```

Now that you've done that, you can redeploy your application. When you go to *http://localhost/*, you'll see the quote application running.

What just happened?

You saw how to set an application to serve the root context in JBoss. With EAR files, declaring the context root can be done in an application-server-independent way. However, with a standalone WAR file, you had to use the *jboss-web.xml* file to declare the context.

Removing the Class Download Service

The last service you'll need to worry about is the class download service. The class download service allows remote RMI clients to download Java classes from the server. It's a nice idea because then you don't have to distribute your server classes to your external clients.

However, leaving the class download service running exposes anything in the server's classpath to external clients. Try accessing *http://localhost:8083/login-config.xml*, or worse yet, *http://localhost:8083/props/jmx-console-users.properties*, to see the potential problems with the class download service.

How do I do that?

To remove the ability to download class files, you need to edit *conf/jboss-service.xml* and remove the jboss:service=WebService MBean. It looks like this:

```
<!-- ======================================================== -->
<!-- Class Loading                                            -->
<!-- ======================================================== -->

<mbean code="org.jboss.web.WebService"
    name="jboss:service=WebService">
    <attribute name="Port">8083</attribute>
    <!-- Should resources and non-EJB classes be downloadable -->
    <attribute name="DownloadServerClasses">true</attribute>
    <attribute name="Host">${jboss.bind.address}</attribute>
    <attribute name="BindAddress">${jboss.bind.address}</attribute>
</mbean>
```

If you do really need the class download service for remote clients, you should at least set DownloadServerClasses to false to restrict the service to supply only EJB-related classes.

What just happened?

You saw how to remove the class download service. If you really need the class download service to facilitate the process of managing external clients, you should set DownloadServerClasses to false to limit the amount of server-side information exposed to clients.

Index

We'd like to hear your suggestions for improving our indexes. Send email to *index@oreilly.com*.

minimal server configuration, 9
monitoring
    applications, 113
    creating monitor, Web
        Console, 121
    email alerts, creating, 125
    MBeans and, 118
      graphing, 119
    snapshots and, 120
MySQL
    JDBC driver code, 49
    setup, 47

O

object mapping, 94
one-to-many relationships, 100
one-to-one relationships, 100
overriding types, 97

P

packaging application, 13
Password attribute, mail server
        authentication, 125
passwords, hashed, 65
persistence
    audit data, 104
    configuration, schema
        management, 91
    object mapping and, 94
    primary keys and, 108
    relationship mapping, 99
primary keys
    generating, 108
      sequential, 109
    persistence and, 108

R

RefreshPeriod attribute
    logging, 79
relational databases
    role data, 64
    security, 63
    user information, 64
relationships
    many-to-many, 100
    mapping, 99
    one-to-many, 100
    one-to-one, 100
relationships element, 100

remove-table flag, 91
role data, relational databases, 64
rolling logfiles, 84
rollout
    class download service, 143
    console management, 129–132
    HTTP Invokers and, 133
    Hypersonic removal, 137
    JMS invoker configuration, 134
    JMX Invoker and, 132
    root web application and, 141
    Tomcat connector
        configuration, 139
root web application, rollout and, 141
run script, bin directory, 3
run.bat file (Windows), 3
running new application, 20
run.sh script (Unix), 3

S

Safari enabled icon, xvi
SAR (service archive) files, 113
schema
    changes, TaskBean priority
        field, 93
    databases, entity beans
        changes, 91
    management, 91
      flags, 91
security
    application security, 68
    domains, defining, 61
    JMX Invoker and, 132
    passwords, hashed, 65
    relational databases, 63
    SSL, enabling, 75
    stacked login modules, 72
    UsersRolesLoginModule, 62
SecurityConf attribute, JMS
        invoker, 135
sequential key generation, 109
server
    configuration
      add/remove services, 11
      all option, 9
      custom, 9
      default, 9
      minimal, 9
      specification, 8
    shut down, 7
ServerInfo MBean, 116

Norman Richards is a JBoss developer at JBoss, Inc., and is a strong believer in the professional open source model which allows him to earn a living creating open source software. He is the coauthor of *XDoclet in Action* and *JBoss 4.0: The Official Guide*. Norman graduated from the University of Texas at Austin and has been happily living in Austin, Texas ever since.

Sam Griffith, Jr. has been doing software development since 1979 and object-oriented development since 1987, starting with MacApp with the MacPIG group at Texas A&M. He transitioned to NeXSTEP, C++, Objective-C, and Smalltalk and did some mentoring in object-oriented development methods. He worked as a mentor and developer with those tools through the 1990s. In 1995, he began working with the first version of Java. In 1996, he and some friends started their own consulting company. That company delivered several commercial Java solutions for Nortel Networks, as well as becoming a Microsoft Solutions Partner in less than one year. In 1997, he taught Java at Southern Methodist University. He then sold his share of the company and went back to consulting, which led to working at Capital One in 1999, where he started selling the architecture team on the idea that Java was mature enough for enterprise use. He next worked on the first J2EE project at Capital One, and that project (case-based credit collections) was one of the first that used a business rules engine together with J2EE.

Since then, Sam has been doing consulting, training, and other odds and ends with Java and other languages, including Smalltalk and Ruby. He is a big fan of dynamic languages and systems. He is currently a developer at Dell, Inc. and a dad (his most important job).

About the Authors

Our look is the result of reader comments, our own experimentation, and feedback from distribution channels. Distinctive covers complement our distinctive approach to technical topics, breathing personality and life into potentially dry subjects.

The *Developer's Notebook* series is modeled on the tradition of laboratory notebooks. Laboratory notebooks are an invaluable tool for researchers and their successors.

The purpose of a laboratory notebook is to facilitate the recording of data and conclusions as the work is being conducted, creating a faithful and immediate history. The notebook begins with a title page that includes the owner's name and the subject of research. The pages of the notebook should be numbered and prefaced with a table of contents. Entries must be clear, easy to read, and accurately dated; they should use simple, direct language to indicate the name of the

Colophon

experiment and the steps taken. Calculations are written out carefully and relevant thoughts and ideas recorded. Each experiment is introduced and summarized as it is added to the notebook. The goal is to produce comprehensive, clearly organized notes that can be used as a reference. Careful documentation creates a valuable record and provides a practical guide for future developers.

Colleen Gorman was the production editor and proofreader, and Audrey Doyle was the copyeditor for *JBoss: A Developer's Notebook*. Genevieve d'Entremont and Claire Cloutier provided quality control. Johnna VanHoose Dinse wrote the index.

Edie Freedman designed the cover of this book. Karen Montgomery produced the cover layout with InDesign CS using the Officina Sans and JuniorHandwriting fonts.

David Futato designed the interior layout with assistance from Edie Freedman. This book was converted by Joe Wizda to FrameMaker 5.5.6 with a format conversion tool created by Erik Ray, Jason McIntosh, Neil Walls, and Mike Sierra that uses Perl and XML technologies. The text font is Adobe Boton; the heading font is ITC Officina Sans; the code font is LucasFont's TheSans Mono Condensed, and the handwriting font is a modified version of JuniorHandwriting, made by Tepid Monkey Foundry and modified by O'Reilly. The illustrations that appear in the book were produced by Robert Romano and Jessamyn Read using Macromedia FreeHand MX and Adobe Photoshop 7. This colophon was written by Colleen Gorman.

Get even more for your money.

Join the O'Reilly Community, and register the O'Reilly books you own. It's free, and you'll get:

- $4.99 ebook upgrade offer
- 40% upgrade offer on O'Reilly print books
- Membership discounts on books and events
- Free lifetime updates to ebooks and videos
- Multiple ebook formats, DRM FREE
- Participation in the O'Reilly community
- Newsletters
- Account management
- 100% Satisfaction Guarantee

Signing up is easy:

1. Go to: oreilly.com/go/register
2. Create an O'Reilly login.
3. Provide your address.
4. Register your books.

Note: English-language books only

To order books online:
oreilly.com/store

For questions about products or an order:
orders@oreilly.com

To sign up to get topic-specific email announcements and/or news about upcoming books, conferences, special offers, and new technologies:
elists@oreilly.com

For technical questions about book content:
booktech@oreilly.com

To submit new book proposals to our editors:
proposals@oreilly.com

O'Reilly books are available in multiple DRM-free ebook formats. For more information:
oreilly.com/ebooks

Spreading the knowledge of innovators   oreilly.com

Have it your way.

Lightning Source UK Ltd.
Milton Keynes UK
UKHW03f1852170918
329072UK00005B/311/P